# Punchi Nona, a Story of Female Education and Village Life in Ceylon

## Samuel Langdon

KANDY

# PUNCHI NONA.

A Story of

## FEMALE EDUCATION

### AND

## VILLAGE LIFE IN CEYLON.

BY THE

REV. S. LANGDON.

London:

T. WOOLMER, 2, CASTLE STREET, CITY ROAD, E.C.;

AND 66, PATERNOSTER ROW, E.C.

1884.

HAYMAN BROTHERS AND LILLY,
PRINTERS,
HATTON HOUSE, 112, FARRINGDON ROAD,
LONDON, E.C.

To MRS. WISEMAN,

AND HER 'BUSY BEES,'

THIS LITTLE STORY OF THE WORK AND

INFLUENCE OF A VILLAGE SCHOOL IN CEYLON

(REPRINTED FROM 'AT HOME AND ABROAD')

IS RESPECTFULLY INSCRIBED,

WITH A GRATEFUL APPRECIATION OF THEIR LABOURS

ON BEHALF OF

FEMALE EDUCATION IN THE EAST,

BY THE AUTHOR.

KANDY, *May 1st*, 1884.

# Contents.

# List of Illustrations.

# PUNCHI NONA.

## CHAPTER I.

### PUNCHI NONA HERSELF.

CEYLON is the scene of the story which I am going to tell you, and Punchi Nona is the name of the girl about whom I am going to write.

Now you must be careful as to how you pronounce this name. If you pronounce it as you do the name of the hero of the

Punch and Judy shows, and anybody from Ceylon should hear you, it would set his teeth on edge, just as the sharpening of a file does yours.   In Ceylon it is considered a dreadful thing to pronounce the letter ʊ in that way; and when English people say Bŭddha, as they often do with a short *u*, instead of *Boodha*, it becomes quite painful to any one who knows anything of Eastern languages.

So, if you say the name at all, you must please pronounce it as if it were written Poonchi Nona, with a long *o* in the second name as well as a long *u* in the first.

So much for the pronunciation.   Now for a word or two about its meaning.   The Singhalese people, and indeed most Oriental people, are very fond of fine names, and if they do not happen to be born with a grand name, they do not hesitate to take one.   For instance, one meets with names 'which being interpreted' mean '*The ruler of the heavens,*' '*The royal lion,*' '*The gem of the earth,*' &c. Well, Punchi Nona's '*gey,*' or family name, was a long one of that kind.   Here it is, but I shall not expect you to remember it or to pronounce it correctly.   You may count the letters if you like—Jayawardene Liyanageywickramasekere. And now add to this Punchi Nona, and you get a name long enough to satisfy anybody. I have met with much longer, and I should not be surprised if Punchi Nona's was really longer, but that was all that I heard of it.

Even Christians think that there is a great deal in a name, and when natives become Christians they generally select for their new name some famous name in history, or the name of some eminent Missionary. They think they may as well have a good name while they are about it. And why shouldn't they ?

But I am writing all this about names in general when I ought to be saying something about this name in particular. Punchi Nona means '*little lady*.' She was not at all what you would call 'a lady' at the time when my story begins; but I hope we shall find, as the story proceeds, that she got to deserve the title afterwards, and it will be my business to try and show you how she got to be a true lady in the best sense of the term.

How do you begin when you are asked to describe a 'little lady' whom you have seen in the Sunday school, or met at a friend's

house ?   Do you not begin with the dress, and
say : 'O, she had such a lovely jacket,
trimmed with beautiful dark lace!'  If you
do not talk like that, I know some little girls
who do. So we will begin with Punchi Nona's
dress.   When I saw her first, she had less in
the way of dress than you can see even in the
pictures of the poor girls as they are sometimes received into 'the Children's Home.'
It was only a piece of cloth bound around the
waist in the form of a skirt, called a 'comboy;' but as the weather is never cold in the
place where Punchi Nona lived, that did not
matter so much.   That was all.  You see it
does not take long to describe her dress, for a
very good reason—she had not much to
describe.   And I am not sorry for it, because,
if she had, I should be sure to make a bungle
of the description.  Why, when she was
dressed in her very best, in her little white
jacket and comboy (skirt), at the Singhalese
New Year festival, her entire costume would
be over-valued at a rupee, or two shillings.
How much does yours cost ?   Wouldn't your
parents like to live in Ceylon ?   Dress in the
class to which Punchi Nona belonged is not
an expensive item.

But she had the most beautiful glossy, black hair I ever saw. And it was all her own of course. Generally she wore her hair tied up in a 'condy,' or knot behind; and when I saw her first it was not tied up with a piece of blue ribbon, such as I have seen around the hair of pretty little English girls, but with an old rag, and that rag was not over clean. And there was such a lot of it when she let it down, as she did on those rare occasions when she took a bath, I dare say a poet would say that it looked like a grand waterfall circling over the black rocks, or something of that kind. As I am not a poet, I must satisfy myself with simple prose.

No; it must be confessed that Punchi Nona was not a little lady at the time referred to. She was just a little 'mudlark,' sitting on a mudbank in front of her father's house. And I believe she liked it. She was unladylike enough to like the mud and the dirt. And, unlike English children who make mud pies, she seemed to think it altogether unnecessary to wash the mud off.

She was not playing at making mud pies, because she had never seen a real pie, and the Singhalese people never eat pies; but I think

she was making mud rice and curry, and she
was trying to make her little baby brother
believe that the sand was the best rice, and
the mud the very best curry that ever was
seen. Baby could not make believe so much,
and was disgusted at the attempts to make
him swallow such nonsense. Babies are
peculiarly unimaginative, you know. You
would not take him for a Singhalese 'Jack
Horner,' 'eating his Christmas pie.'

She was very dirty, but she had, as I have
said, the most beautiful black hair, and she
had also two of the brightest black eyes I
ever saw. Anybody who has ever seen Singhalese children will understand that. Altogether she was as bright a little mudlark as
one could expect to see even in that country
where such birds are plentiful.

I stood looking at her as she tried to per-
suade baby that he was exceedingly stupid to
refuse to taste her richly flavoured curry and
tenderly boiled rice. And baby sputtered and
kicked. He had no imagination worth speaking of. They were not aware that I was
looking, so I had plenty of time for seeing
what sort of a girl she was. And when at
last she did turn her eyes on me, I felt at a

glance that this little muddy creature might be raised to a real, bright 'little lady,' and, higher still, might be raised to a real, bright angel of God. You will remember that story in your English History which tells of a Roman bishop called Gregory who had the same idea about some English children that he saw at Rome, at a time when English children—the little 'Angles'—were as heathen and uncivilized as the majority of the children in Ceylon are to-day. This little historical reference will, perhaps, help you to feel thankful for what the Christian faith has done for England, while it will give you a hint of what it may do for Ceylon.

Now, I must warn you beforehand that this is not going to be a sort of Ceylon Cinderella story, and I am not going to tell a tale of how a beggar-maid became a princess; but it is going to be a story of great rise in life all the same. I must finish this chapter here, or I shall tell you all about the story to begin with, and you know that would never do.

# CHAPTER II.

## SOME OF PUNCHI NONA'S RELATIONS.

WHERE was I at the end of the last chapter? O, I know! I was standing near the door of Punchi Nona's father's house, watching her attempts to make her baby brother believe in her mud rice and curry. She held him to her side with one arm, while she supported the make-believe rice and curry on a piece of plantain leaf in the other.

I must stand here a little longer while I describe baby to you. And this will be an opportunity for you to get to know something about Singhalese babies. Baby is, I can assure you, one of the most important and influential of Punchi Nona's relatives. He is thought a great deal of in the house, first, because he is a boy, and second, because he is the only boy. Punchi Nona is given to understand that she is of very little importance in life, compared with her baby brother. The astrologer has told her father that he will be a great man in the village some day, and that he will own several houses, and a great many cocoa-nut trees. And Punchi Nona is told that she must be always doing what she can for the comfort of this wonderful child.

I could describe Punchi Nona's dress easily, because she had so little to describe. The task is a much easier one with baby, because he has nothing to describe. All babies of that class go naked until they are about two years old. Baby had had his head shaven some time before with a great deal of ceremony. As is the rule on such occasions, a religious festival had been held, and the village astrologer had said some wonderful things about the boy, which made the father and mother feel very proud. Punchi Nona had thought that it was a lot of fuss to make over such a little hair. And this baby was very pretty in the eyes of his father and mother. I cannot say that that was my idea. Punchi Nona thought him pretty sometimes, but at this particular moment she thought he was the ugliest baby she had ever seen, because he despised the rice and curry which she had prepared with such care.

She had no cradle to put him in when he was tired and wanted sleep, but on such occasions she would lay him on a little mat on the mud floor of the house, or she would sit down and beat his little head against her knees as she had seen her mother do, making the head keep time with some monotonous Singhalese lullaby she had been taught to sing. Probably something of this kind:—

> *' Theng lamaya lamaya*
> *Niddhaganta yannawa.*
> *Theng yakshaya, yakshaya,*
> *Langa nethi ennawa.'*

> ' Now the child, the child
> Is going to sleep.
> Now the demon, the demon
> Will not come near.'

It is not nearly so nice a way of being put to sleep as being rocked in a cradle. I think I would rather be the famous ' Baby Bunting on the tree top ' than Punchi Nona's little brother under such circumstances. But it is ' the Singhalese fashion,' and the babies do not seem to object to it very much. I am sure I should.

Then when baby awoke there was a splendid nursery for him in the mudbank just outside the door, which we have already seen, and before which we have been standing so long. It would not have done, however, to have left baby out of a description of Punchi Nona's relatives.

As soon as Punchi Nona saw me, she dropped her make-believe plate of rice and curry, laid hold of baby, bent her little body in a graceful curve towards the right side, set baby astride on the left, the usual method of carrying either babies or pitchers with Singhalese women, and would have rushed straight indoors with her precious burden, but the mudbank was in the way, and Punchi Nona's foot caught in the bank, and a great change came over the quiet scene and the playful group which we have been so long and so deliberately watching. Punchi Nona fell head foremost, and baby got thrown sprawling some little distance, with nearly as much violence as Baby Bunting experienced in his celebrated fall.

When English babies fall they invariably cry, and Singhalese babies are just the same. If they do not scream, the case is considered serious. Punchi Nona's little brother screamed with all his baby might. This was a good sign. He was not dead at any rate. But his poor sister had fared much worse. She had struck her head against a large flat stone on which she had been preparing her make-believe curry, and the blow was so heavy, that it had brought the blood down her cheeks. Poor little thing! She did not scream at all, but immediately on my raising her, she rushed to the baby, who was evidently disgusted because I had given my attention to his sister before him.

Poor little Punchi Nona! Forgetful of her own hurt, she, with tears in her eyes, tried to soothe baby, and the more she tried to soothe him, the more vigorously did baby scream and kick.

I was trying to wash Punchi Nona's wound with a handful of water from the brook, which ran by the side of the road through the village, when a woman appeared in the door-way, attracted from a gossip with a neighbour, or awakened out of a nap, by the screams of the baby. She had a very determined look on her face. She had a stick in her hand. When women appear with sticks in their hands on such occasions, you know that they mean something. They mean to use them. And

she meant to use that stick. She had heard
the cries of baby, and she knew that somebody would deserve the stick. It was Punchi
Nona, of course, who was to be punished, but
when she saw me she was rather taken aback.
An Englishman was not by any means an every-
day sight in the village, and to see an Englishman bathing the face of a little village girl was
most unusual. Nevertheless she retained the
stick, and after the first surprise was over, she
looked as if she would like to lay it on my
back. It is not at all pleasant to see a woman
with a stick in her hand. She snatched the
baby away from Punchi Nona's arm, and began
scolding in language so fluent, that I could
not understand her; but when she saw that
her daughter had been wounded, she stopped
very suddenly. But she still held the stick.
Need I say that the woman with the stick was
Punchi Nona's mother ?

Punchi Nona felt better. She rose to her
feet, and looking at me with her big, bright
eyes, which were all the brighter because of
the tears which were still lingering in them,
she said, and I thought she said it very sweetly,
, Bohoma isthuthi mahatmaya, theng sanee-
pay.' 'Very many thanks, Sir; I feel better now.'

After this I will try not to bother you with many Singhalese words, but write my story in such a way as little English boys and girls will understand.

I must say a few words more about Punchi Nona's mother. She did not look very beautiful at first when I saw her. Angry women with sticks in their hands very rarely do, any more than angry children do. But when she saw that Punchi Nona had been hurt and that baby had not, the expression of motherly kindness, added to what were really fine features, made her look, so I thought, quite pretty. For good looks, you know, depend greatly on expression, and therefore on tempers and dispositions all over the world, whether in Singhalese women or English, in Singhalese children or English.

She looked very much like Punchi Nona, only her eyes were not so bright. She was dressed a little better than her daughter. She wore not only the skirt or *comboy* but also a little white jacket. Her garments were, no doubt, originally white. That is what I mean by saying that the jacket was white. At present it was of that peculiar drab colour which speaks of the rare occurrence of washing day.

When she went to the temple, however, with her offering of flowers, she would always put on spotlessly clean garments, and the folds of her *condy*, or chignon, were gathered up by a silver hair-pin. This hair-pin often indicates the wealth of the wearer. Sometimes it is gold studded with precious stones; sometimes, gold without any gems; and, oftener still, it is a plain bit of silver. Punchi Nona's mother wore one of silver on such great occasions. But on the occasion to which I refer she had nothing of the kind. She had no adornment whatever. Or if it is true that 'beauty unadorned is adorned the most,' well, these simple people were more richly adorned than royalty itself.

For what I have said of the simplicity of the costumes of Marihami, Punchi Nona's mother, and of Punchi Nona herself, will apply to the costume of the father, who presently appeared on the scene, dragging a net after him, which he was intending to mend, for Punchi Nona's father was a fisherman. And this was his boat which he and his partners had brought up on the beach near the back of the house, leaving the sail spread to be dried. A curious boat, is it not?

You would say so if you saw the real boat—
all made of the cocoa-nut palm, and tied
together (not a nail in it) with coir yarn, the
rope made from the husk of the cocoa-nut.
And you would say it was the swiftest boat
you ever saw, if you could be in it, as I have

been, when it has been running before a
monsoon breeze, and the men have stood out
on the funny outrigger, which you see in the
picture, in order to steady it.

Punchi Nona's father was dressed in a
skirt fastened round the waist, like his

daughter, and that was all. And, indeed, if you had not been told, you might have judged from his dress and appearance that he was a woman; for he not only wore his hair in the form of a chignon, but he also wore, as nearly all Singhalese men do, a tortoise-shell comb circling round the top of his head. Gregoris Appu—that was his ordinary name, the other, the long one, was only for special occasions—on hearing the story of the fall, took the baby up very tenderly into his arms, and asked me if I would come in.

Now I have described the immediate relatives of Punchi Nona; and the invitation to come inside gives me an opportunity of describing the house.

The house was as simple in its way as were the garments of the people. There was not much of it to describe. It had been built as most of the poorer class of natives build their houses in Ceylon. They had built the roof first. They had put a roof on a dozen poles, a roof of thatch, and then built walls up according to the number of rooms required. There were three rooms in this house, one tolerably large, while the other two were more like the rooms of a doll's house, they were

so small.    Then there was a pretty large
verandah behind, where the cooking was per-
formed, where Gregoris Appu slept when he
was not out fishing, while Marihami and
Punchi Nona pounded the rice.    The front
verandah, such as it was, was made a sort of
shop, in which Marihami sold rice-cakes
and plantains.

The floor of the house all through was of
hard mud.    There was a table in the big
room, which was called 'the visitors' room,'
and there were also two chairs; but as the
room was seldom used, except when visitors
came, there was not much danger of the
furniture being worn out by hard usage.    This,
with a low wooden couch on which Gregoris
slept, and a small box where the trinkets
and clothes were kept, formed the household
furniture.    You could buy it all at an auction
for ten shillings, and you would probably
think it a bad bargain at that.

This was Punchi Nona's father's house.
Gregoris is sitting in the front now, pretend-
ing to be keeping away the crows from the
rice-cakes, but crows are very cunning and
very quick, and will carry off the finest,
fattest cake of the lot before Gregoris can

say the Singhalese of ' Jack Robinson,' whatever that may be. You must get up early and look very sharp all day, Gregoris, if you would be a match for the crow.

I wanted to say something also about the village; but we must get on with the story,

and perhaps I shall be able to tell you a little about the village as we go along.

It was in ' the visitors' room ' of Gregoris Appu's small house that I unfolded my scheme for Female Education in Nidigamma. Nidigamma was the name of the village. I will tell you more about that name by-and-by. It had pained me very much in my occasional visits to this large and populous village to see the neglected state of the children. It was true that there was a school for boys at some distance from the village, but there was nothing being done for the girls. And the greater part of the boys preferred rolling about in the road, or sleeping under a tree, to the discipline of the school.

Some of you have read or heard or seen something of the good work being done by Dr. Stephenson in connection with the 'Children's Home' in Bonner Road, London. You will have heard what he says of the dreadful state in which he finds 'City Arabs' at times. In most of the out-of-the-way villages of Ceylon that condition of things is general. And what is worse, the people too often appear contented with the destitution and ignorance in which they live.

Our schools in these places might be called 'Ragged Schools,' if the children had clothes enough to make them look ragged. And here and there a boarding-school partakes of the character of a 'Children's Home.' Many a village have I passed through, sighing

and fretting that I have not been in a position
to establish such a ' Children's Home ' in it for
the elevation of the boys and girls above its
corruptions.

We know what idleness and ignorance
will lead to in England, and it is the same in
Ceylon and all the world over. The children
learn to talk in a language which you would
shudder to hear, if you could understand it,
and which your parents would not let you
hear for the world; language not the less
sinful because spoken in Singhalese. And the
ignorance and depravity of these poor heathen
people is none the less because the people
wear dark skins. In the midst of all
the heathen degradation we often meet with
tokens of good disposition, kindliness, and
courtesy in manners which ought to put some
people I have seen in this Christian kingdom
to shame.

And this is to my mind a very strong
reason why we should do all that we possibly
can to raise them, by means of preaching the
Gospel, and by a Christian education. It
will pay amongst a people who are so suscep-
tible of kindness, and so quick at recognising
what is really good and true. We have

found in many cases, that in villages where
we have had very few open converts to
Christianity through our work, yet the village life has been invariably elevated. People leave off many of their corrupt ways and
bad habits.  The old home life is soon seen
to be inconsistent with what the children
learn in the school, and the children often
teach their parents how to make their homes
better.  Many cases have been known where
a large village has been entirely reformed
by the presence of a girls' school.

It was because I knew all this that I was
so anxious to establish a girls' school in
Nidigamma, and that brings me back to
Punchi Nona.  I am sure to wander a little
if I get on this topic, for the great need
which exists for such institutions is a matter
of deep feeling with me in reference to Mission work.

Some kind friends in England had pro-
mised me help in this matter.  It was a
Sunday school, the scholars of which had
by some means got to be deeply interested
in our work in Ceylon, and had arranged
amongst themselves to raise £12 a year,
which would be sufficient for the support

of an ordinary village school. You will see by-and-by what a very great benefit the generous children in the English Sunday school were thus able to confer on the girls of Nidigamma, and, indeed, on the whole village.

And now I will conclude this chapter by just mentioning that I know lots of villages like Nidigamma without schools of any kind, where we could get similar results if you could get us the £12 a year.

# CHAPTER III.

## THE EDUCATION SCHEME IS UNFOLDED TO
## GREGORIS APPU.

THERE were many villages needing a girls' school, as there are still, but I thought Nidigamma needed it most; and just then, as there was no Christian agency at work in the neighbourhood, it seemed to offer a good field for Mission work. I told Gregoris Appu what I intended doing, and asked him to let Punchi Nona be our first pupil.

You know what a look of surprise is, of course, but you never saw a look of greater surprise than Gregoris Appu gave me when I made this proposition.

'What, Sir, a school for girls! Why, what good can come of a school for girls?'

'Now, Gregoris, just think for a moment of the advantage it would be to you and your family now if Marihami had received some education in early life. She would have been taught to sew, and I need not tell you what

an advantage that would be even in a house
like yours. It is not often that you want
any writing done; but when you do, would
it not be much better to have somebody in
your own house who could do it, than to
have to go to the notary?'

Gregoris shook his head. This argument
was making very little impression on him.
He had only had three or four letters written for him in all his life.

'Then think of the pleasure it would be to
you to get somebody to read to you. She could
read to you the *Kirana*, and you would then
get all the news.'

Gregoris looked interested.

'And when you are selling fish, sometimes you make mistakes, as you do also in
buying rice—mistakes which you would not
make if you had somebody about you who
knew a little of arithmetic.'

Gregoris Appu became quite wide-awake.

'By-and-by, you will have to think, as
all fathers who have daughters have to think,
about some sort of a dowry for Punchi Nona,
in order to secure a marriage. The best
dowry in the world that you could give her
would be a good education. The young men

are getting educated now and are beginning
to value that kind of thing. There is nothing
that will make a girl so marriageable as
such an education as we propose. I know
very well that you have not much to give her.'

'*Appooyi*, Sir; I believe you!'

I talked to him about English girls and
their education. He could not understand
the English people thinking so much of mere
girls. He had thought that when the wonderful baby grew up he would try and send
him to school somewhere; but the idea of
educating Punchi Nona had never entered
his mind.

'If I send her to your school, will she
become like English girls? Will she talk
English? and will she get white?'

It was impossible to resist a smile at the
simplicity with which Gregoris discussed the
great question of female education. His
next question was, 'Will it change her religion?'

'I cannot say; I hope it will! What
will your religion do for her? What has it
done for Marihami, or for you? Where are
the schools established by Buddhist priests
for the education of women? Your priest

will tell you, if he is honest, that women are spoken of in the Buddhist scriptures as hardly superior to the lower animals. He could tell you too that the great Buddha himself made a law that women were not to be allowed to hear the Buddhist scriptures read " unless in the company of some very wise men," because their intellects were too low to understand them. Now tell me candidly, Gregoris, don't you think Marihami's intellect is just as good as yours ? '

Gregoris looked a curious assent, though he didn't like to put it into words. I went on :—

'Buddhism would make them all slaves. In Christian schools they are taught, not only to become useful in the life in the house, but also to become fit companions and equals of their husbands. They learn things which will tend to make the home happy.'

'No; our priests have not done that for us. And yet I have been told by our priest that very learned English gentlemen praise our Buddhist religion very highly.'

'That is because they have not seen it as we see it here, in such places as this, quiet and content in the midst of general ignorance and debasement.'

Gregoris got puzzled, and began combing his hair with the black tortoise-shell comb which adorned his head, to see if he could get his ideas into clearer shape.   This failing, he fell back on the old stock phrase, ' Well, it was good enough for my father and grand-father, and it will do for me.'

' But it was *not* good enough for your father and grandfather, and it is not good enough for you.   It is not good at all.   Your father and grandfather would have been much better men if they had gone to school.   And you would probably have been living in a much better house than this, and under much better circumstances, if they had.'

This is something like the way in which we talked.   In those days it was difficult to get the people to see the necessity for educating their girls.   Education of any kind in the villages was altogether at a discount.   I am glad to say that it is not so now.   Earnest entreaties come to us from the villagers themselves for the establishment of such schools, which we are often obliged to refuse for want of the funds to build a school house and support a teacher. For, as in the case of Nidigamma, the people are often too poor to give us much help.

Gregoris Appu went on combing his hair for some time in deep thought. At last he said, 'Well, Sir, I wish you success; and as you have not got the schoolroom built, you may have the use of this till the proper room is ready.'

I think Gregoris liked being taken into confidence in so important a matter. The room was not all that one could wish for a school, as you may well believe from the description given in the last chapter, but it was better than nothing; and as I wanted to lose no time, I gladly accepted Gregoris' kind offer.

I went around to the families in the place, talking with them in much the same way about the necessity for sending their girls to school, and before the day was over we had promises of about twenty girls as pupils.

We sent a *tom-tom* beater (a man with a kind of small drum) through the village to announce that the school would be opened on the next Monday in the house of Gregoris Appu.

I thought I should be able to tell you about the opening; but that must be left for another chapter, when perhaps we shall see something more of Punchi Nona.

# CHAPTER IV.

## THE OPENING DAY.

THE opening day of the Nidigamma girls' school was a day to be remembered. Gregoris Appu, Punchi Nona's father, had his house decorated as it had never been decorated since he and Marihami first came there to live. There was an arch over the front door adorned with cocoa-nuts and plantains and beautiful mosses and graceful leaves of the sago palm. I wish I could give you a picture of it, but I was never good at sketching, and you, little boys and girls, know so much about drawing now-a-days that you would be sure to see flaws in any poor picture that I could produce. But that arch with the bright-looking face of Gregoris, who stood in the doorway to welcome any children that might come, was a scene that would be worth the attention of any artist in the Royal Academy.

Punchi Nona, as you may imagine, was very anxious indeed and full of tremulous excitement. Baby, of course, knew what it

was all about, and looked as if he thought
his opinion ought to be asked about everything. He seemed to realise that this event
was one of the responsibilities of life, and became profoundly quiet in consequence. And
Punchi Nona was not sorry that baby took
the affair so seriously. Gregoris Appu moves
out into the street to have another look at the
front of the house before the arrival of the
Missionary and the teacher. Well, it did
look as if no girl in Nidigamma ought to be
able to resist the temptation to come to
school. Those cocoa-nuts and plantains!
If they were meant to symbolise the sweets
of learning, going to school must be the
pleasantest thing in the world. Then there
were those wonderful English words over the
door! Gregoris could not understand them.
They had been done by a clever boy in the
village who had learnt a little English in a
school at some distance. To Gregoris they
were as mysterious as the inscriptions on the
old Assyrian monuments in the British
Museum are to us, but they ought to be
more impressive on that account. And there
they were done up in such lovely moss. It
was something like this—

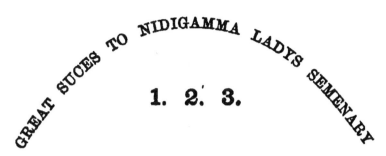

# WELCOME.

You will know, of course, that I am not responsible for the spelling, nor the arrangement of the words. That was the work of Ratnaike, the clever boy referred to above; and of course he was responsible for the grand name under which the new school was announced. For my part I was glad when the letters fell, but it did not matter much, as very few of the Nidigamma people saw anything amiss in the words on the arch. On the contrary, many a father felt proud as he led his little girls into the schoolroom at the thought that the time would come when the mysterious words would be as clear to his daughters as they were to Ratnaike, who had studied in the English school.

An attempt was made to open the school with singing, but as the only persons present

RATNAIKE.

who could sing were the Missionary and the teacher, and as all the dogs in the village began to howl on hearing the unwonted sounds, the attempt soon broke down. You can imagine a Sunday school opening with a hymn sung only by the superintendent and one of the teachers. After an earnest prayer for the divine blessing on the movement, the Minister introduced the teacher, a Mrs. de Silva, a widow, a good Christian lady, who in her youth had been educated in one of our Mission schools. He told the parents present what the object of the Society was in establishing the school; that they meant to do all that they possibly could towards educating the girls for the necessities of this life and for a better life beyond. He hoped that before long they would see the value of the school to the village, and would give their best assistance to the building of a new schoolroom. He concluded by tendering the thanks of the Society to Gregoris Appu for the loan of the room; and Gregoris began to feel that he was rising in the world to have put the great Society under such an obligation to himself.

The first formal business after the introductory remarks had been made was the

enrolling of the names of the scholars. This
was done in a new register laid out on a little
old second-hand dressing-table, which did
duty for a teacher's desk. The first name was
that of Punchi Nona, who was brought
forward to the desk by Gregoris. There was
a column in the register for the ages of the
pupils, and the question as to Punchi Nona's
age seemed to plunge Gregoris into great
difficulty. He scratched his head and tried
hard to answer the question, but it was of no
use: he could not for the life of him guess
how many years it was since Punchi Nona
had first seen the light. 'Bless me,' he said,
'she isn't as old as I am, I know. Well now,
should you think she was twenty?'

This enlivened if it did not enlighten those
present, and at last Gregoris gave it up and
appealed to Marihami. She was in the back
verandah. The truth was, that Marihami did
not much approve of the school, and she had
already said some hard things to Gregoris for
offering the room without having first talked
it over with his wife. Of course, Gregoris
ought to have done that, but I fancy he knew
pretty well that Marihami would mention it
to the priest, and that there would be con-

siderable opposition if he did. Marihami
could throw very little light on the matter of
Punchi Nona's age, and the result was, that
the teacher made a guess, which, I dare say,
was very near the truth; and our little friend
was entered as :—

'Punchi Nona; age 12.'

I wish I had a portrait of her as she stood
there by the desk while her age was being
discussed; but, as I told you just now, I am
no artist, and there was no photographer in
Nidigamma just then.  She would have made
a very pretty picture, she was looking so
bright, and neat, and clean.  Ratnaike, the
clever boy who made the wonderful English
letters, and came to see the school begin,
thought he had never seen so pretty a girl in
his life before.

As soon as the names were all entered
(there were twenty in all) the parents and
visitors retired, and the 'Nidigamma Ladies'
Seminary,' as Ratnaike had called it in his
grand English style, entered on its regular
duties.

It was easy to classify the pupils, because
not one of them could read or write.  They
were therefore all put in one class, with

Punchi Nona at the top of it. The first lesson was a Scripture lesson, and consisted of a reading from the Gospels, and explanations by the teacher. Punchi Nona had never heard anything like it before, and she determined that she would soon learn to read that beautiful book for herself.

Poor Punchi Nona! she had no idea of the difficulties in the way.

The whole school was just one alphabet class; and I do think the Singhalese alphabet is much harder than ours is. There are so many letters, and there are some very little changes in the shapes of the letters which make a great difference in the sounds. We had no idea of teaching English for a long time to come. We remembered the old doggerel—

'Let every foreign tongue alone
Till you can read and write your own.'

And so we told the children, who were anxious to learn English at once, that they must at least learn to read a simple book in Singhalese before they tried the English alphabet. We told them what book we should require them to read, and that as soon as they reached that standard they should be promoted to an Anglo-vernacular class, and we would see which could reach it first. I think Punchi Nona made up her mind to be the first to reach that proud position.

It was two or three days after the school had commenced that my wife and I came down to the village and looked in at the school to see how they were getting on. The school was already doing some good work, for there were twenty little girls all neatly dressed— thinly of course. There was hardly a girl present whose clothes you could not buy for a shilling, or even sixpence. In some cases they were ragged, but they were all clean, which was a very good thing; for hitherto they had never considered it necessary to be clean except on bathing days.

In looking around the schoolroom I noticed that one of the girls had turned her back on the school and was hanging her head over an A B C book and sobbing violently. It was Punchi Nona. 'Why, how is this, my child? What are you crying for?' I asked.

'O, Sir! the teacher said Jesus Christ would make all this hard learning easy if we asked Him. And I have been asking

Him all the day; and when you came in I thought it was He coming, and it wasn't. O my! O my!'

I tried to explain to her what the teacher meant, and left her in some degree comforted with what little assistance I could give her.

Baby Gregoris had ceased to look on the school in the serious, philosophic manner which he had assumed on the day of the opening, trying to make people believe that he was the wisest and most thoughtful child that ever lived. He thought it was fine fun to have so many girls to tease. Punchi Nona was all very well, but she was only one; now there were twenty, and young Gregoris liked variety. He preferred school even to the mudbank before the door. A favourite trick of his was to pull at the little strips of cloth with which the girls had tied their hair in knots behind, until it all fell down on their shoulders and gave them a great deal of trouble to gather it up again. He would sometimes get hold of a book and pretend to be very studious. He secured Punchi Nona's book in this way on the day that we were there, and, after reading it in his way very thoughtfully for some time, deliberately tore

it up with a look which intimated that it was
unworthy the attention of so profound a scholar as he was.   And any attempt to interfere
with his recreations brought all his screaming
power into play.  And this would bring Marihami into the room, saying she did not know
what a school was fit for if it could not keep
a baby quiet.  She did not approve of the
school, and saw no reason why Punchi Nona
should learn to read.  We can excuse poor
Marihami. She was a dark-minded Buddhist,
and she was influenced very much by a relative of hers, a demon priest, of whom we shall
perhaps  hear  more  by-and-by.   All  this
inclined  me  to  the  opinion  that  Gregoris
Appu's visitors'-room was not the best place
for  the  Nidigamma  girls'  school, and  I
resolved that as soon as I could get the £15
required  it  should  be  transferred  to a more
suitable building.

# CHAPTER V.

### THE DEMON PRIEST.

I DO not want to frighten you, but did you ever see an uglier old Guy Fawkes than that which heads this chapter? Of course it is not really a Guy Fawkes, but I fancy the hideous mask will remind you at once of the exhibitions in the streets on the fifth of November. It is not a picture of the demon priest to whom I made some allusion in my last chapter, but it is a picture of one of the masks which is used in one of his ceremonies.

You would not think there was anything specially attractive in a man who could make a 'Guy' of himself with a thing like that wooden mask, would you?  But Marihami thought this cousin of hers one of the most handsome men in the village.  He was certainly a man of considerable influence in the place.

You are not to understand from the heading of this chapter that the priest was a demon. What you are to understand is, that he took the leading part in the demon-worshipping ceremonies, which are sadly too common in the villages of Ceylon.

The lower classes in Ceylon, and such people as Punchi Nona's friends, are not very good Buddhists, although they would not like to hear me say so.  They are mostly demon-worshippers as well as Buddhists, and they know a great deal more about the religion of the demon priest than they do about the religion of Buddha.  Buddhism is bad enough, but demon worship is a great deal worse. People become in time very much like the things they worship, and you may judge pretty clearly of the characters of a people by the character of the beings they worship. I do not mean to say that the Singhalese people are as bad as the demons they stand in such dread of, but you can understand how very degrading the worship of such evil spirits must be.

But the demons worshipped by these people are not all bad. Some of them are like the fairies that you read about in some of your children's books. Perhaps you have read Charles Kingsley's book about the *Water Babies.* If you have not, I hope you very soon will, and you will say it is one of the nicest books you ever read.

The Singhalese people have stories about fairies, too—water fairies as well as land fairies —only they regard these stories as true, and not parables like Kingsley's beautiful story, teaching very excellent lessons if people would only learn them.

It would be hard to find any good teaching in some of the Singhalese fairy stories; but some of them have not got much harm in them. And that is saying a great deal for a Singhalese story.

But we must get on with our story, or you will be saying that they must be tedious if they are anything like this ; and, you know, I should feel rather queer if I heard you say that.

Gregoris junior (I scarcely like to call him 'Baby Gregoris' now, because he is two years older than when we saw him last, although he has lots of babyish ways still)—Gregoris junior did not think Punchi Nona's story at all tedious, as he lay stretched out on the floor of the back verandah at full length, with his head resting on his hands, listening to the story his sister was telling him; a story she had read in a schoolbook, an English school-book, at the Nidigamma girls' school.

Gregoris' full length was two feet and a half; but he had an idea that it was much longer. Babies—I beg his pardon—'juveniles' are very conceited, you know, especially when they are 'only sons,' like Gregoris, and have sisters to wait on them and do all sorts of things for them, like Punchi Nona.

You can fancy how deeply interested Gregoris was when I tell you that he had left the mudbank, where we made our first acquaintance with him, and his make-believe rice and curry, to listen to his sister.

'Once there was '—that's how all the nice

stories begin, you know, in England as well
as in Ceylon—'Once there was,' said Punchi
Nona, 'in a country on the other side of the
great sea, where the sun sets, a beautiful
man.'

'A booful man,' said Gregoris, 'where
sun sets.'

'Well, the sun does not set there exactly,
but it was over *that* way,' and Punchi Nona
pointed with her finger towards the west. 'And
He was so kind, nobody was ever so kind as He
was. He was always trying to do good to
people, and was very fond of little children.'

'Didn't He care for big boys like me, then?'
said Gregoris.

'Yes, He cared for everybody, for people
of all sizes; and teacher says that He cared
quite as much for girls as He did for boys.'

'No, not weally and tooly ?'

'Yes, really and truly. I heard Uncle
Jacobis tell father the other day, when they
were talking about our girls' school, that the
Buddhist priests were forbidden to preach
Buddha's doctrine to women, because they
were so foolish, and didn't know so much as
men. But this beautiful man, He didn't think
so. He didn't think the women were at all

stupider than men; and from the stories I have read the women seemed to understand Him a deal better than the men did. I'll tell you about that some day.'

'You don't think that booful man would like you so well as me, Punchi Nona?'

'He would not like either if we were not good.'

'Wouldn't He like Ratnaike, then, the big, clever boy who knows English so well? Was that booful man English?'

'No, He was not English at all, He was not a white Europe man, but He belonged to Asia, He was Asiatic, like we are. But teacher says people do not think about that when they speak of Him, because He belongs to all the world, to everybody, and not to any one place. When you come to learn geography, you will know what Asiatic means. You know I took the geography prize at the examination the other day, and I know lots of things.'

'But where's the story? You said, "Once there was," and didn't tell me no story.'

'Yes, I forgot that! Well, once upon a time there was a poor boy in that country very ill, O! so bad, you never saw anybody so bad ; he was possessed of a demon.   Sarnalis, the *kapua* (demon priest), says that mother is possessed because she is so ill ; but teacher says that is not true, and that the ceremony, the devil dance they are going to hold to-morrow evening, is very sinful.'

' I like see debbil dance,' said Gregoris.

' We must not like to see wicked things ; but this poor boy's father was very sorry, and I think he felt the pain nearly as much as the boy.'

' Was that boy big like me ? ' said Gregoris, looking back over his full length (two feet and a half).

' I think he was bigger.  You are not very big, you know.  The father of the boy went to the doctors, and they couldn't do anything.  Then he took the boy to some of the followers of the beautiful man, and they tried to cast out the demon, but they couldn't. And then, while they were there wondering what could be done, the people began to shout, " The wonderful man is coming. Here he is ! "  And there the beautiful man was coming down the side of the hill, and he was looking more beautifuller than ever. His face was shining most glorious.'

'Most glojus,' said Gregoris.

'You must be quiet, or I'll stop. When the beautiful man came near, the bad spirit got very much afraid, and he was most about mad, because he knew he would have to fly away, and he didn't like to go away; and then the father cried, and asked the beautiful man to make his child well. And he spoke to him so kind. And then the bad spirit came out, but the poor boy was so weak that he couldn't stand; but the beautiful man took him by the hand and helped him along. He wasn't a bit ashamed to walk by the poor little boy and lead him by the arm.'

'What was the booful man called?'

'He was called JESUS, and that means "*one who saves.*" Isn't that a beautiful name?'

'Booful name, booful man!' said Gregoris.

'O my! O my!' shouted Punchi Nona. 'Look, look!' and she pointed to the doorway, where a man stood with his face covered in the ugly mask with which this chapter is headed.

As you will have understood from the dialogue between the sister and brother, poor

Marihami, Punchi Nona's mother, was very ill. Like most of the Singhalese people, Marihami believed that every sickness was produced by some evil spirit, and she had called in the demon priest to arrange for a ceremony which, as she thought, would compel the spirit to cease tormenting her; and that was what had brought the priest to the house that afternoon. Punchi Nona was frightened on seeing the mask. Gregoris was delighted, and thought what a fine thing it must be to be a demon priest to be able to frighten people as he did.

Sarnalis was not a pleasant man to look at even when his mask was off. His face had a habit of going into disagreeable contortions. It was no wonder that Punchi Nona kept out of his way as much as possible.

You will have guessed from what has gone before that Punchi Nona has altered very much since our last chapter. She has indeed, and she is also greatly improved. The demon priest told Marihami that he should very much like to have her for a daughter-in-law. His son would succeed him and take to his profession some day, and he thought they could not do better than arrange for a mar-

E

riage between them. This will not seem strange to you when I tell you that marriages are nearly always arranged by the parents of the parties, and that Singhalese girls are often married when they are very young, sometimes when they are not much older than Punchi Nona.

But this would be very dreadful for Punchi Nona, and it was doubtful whether Gregoris Appu, her father, would consent to the arrangement. I wanted to tell you more about the priest and his son, but I have given you quite enough for one chapter.

# CHAPTER VI.

## THE DEVIL CEREMONY.

**I** FORGOT to tell you in the last chapter that the conversation recorded there between Punchi Nona and her brother was not carried on in English. The conversation was the English equivalent for the Singhalese which they talked.

Punchi Nona and Gregoris junior soon got deeply interested in the preparations which were being made for the devil ceremony. Gregoris thought there was nothing in the world so grand as being a demon priest; and although his sister did not share his views in that respect, she could not help feeling greatly interested in the beautiful little arches which were erected in the compound, or garden, and the decorations of palm-leaves that were thrown over the arches. The demon priest had been there the greater part of the day to see that all the arrangements were properly carried out, and Punchi Nona had taken the opportunity of telling him what

E 2

she thought of the whole affair. It was wicked and sinful to believe that evil spirits had more power than the good God. Such cruel ceremonies as he practised must be displeasing to God, and for her part she should pray earnestly to God for her mother's recovery; and the priest was not to think that his charms and dancing had done it, if Marihami got better, as she trusted she would.

The demon priest laughed and said: 'That's the result of this English schooling, Punchi Nona. It makes people conceited, and they lose all reverence for their elders and betters. I cannot think what Gregoris Appu was about in sending you to school. It isn't right or natural that girls should be taught to read.'

My little English readers will not agree with the priest, I am sure, but will think with me that the school has had a very blessed influence on our young friend Punchi Nona. It was worth all the money and all the trouble spent on the school to see such a spirit growing in the girl as she displayed on the occasion of the devil ceremony.

Punchi Nona had tried to prevail on her father to give up the ceremony, using the

THE DEVIL CEREMONY.

arguments she had learnt at school. Gregoris Appu was in a fix. He liked Punchi Nona, and was getting to like her better every day. She was becoming quite an authority with him, and he had half a mind to shut out the ceremony; but, as he had told his daughter, it was an old custom, and Marihami wished it to take place. If he prevented it and she should die, he would feel sorry all his days.

So the ceremony took place. It began at about eight o'clock in the evening. It was a fine moonlight night, and a great many people, nearly all Nidigamma, including the dogs, who seemed to take a wonderful interest in what was going on, had assembled themselves in the spacious yard at the back of the house.

Poor Marihami was brought out looking wofully thin and haggard, and laid down on a mat on the floor of the verandah. At the head of her bed an ugly image was placed, supposed to represent the demon of the fever from which Marihami was suffering. A fowl was then tied to one of her feet. Then her relative, the demon priest, came out from a beautiful little booth, decorated with mosses and strips of the sago palm. His object just then seemed to be to make as much noise as he possibly could. Nobody could understand a word that he said, and nobody expected to understand it. Some foolish people think it a grand thing to use big English words that are hard to be understood when they are talking, and I think these poor Singhalese people thought that the words of the demon priest were all the better and likely to be more powerful with the spirits because they could not understand them. The priest did not understand them himself; but that did not matter much to him so long as the people were not acquainted with that fact. Do you know what the awful word ' ALDIBORONTHOSKY- PHOSHOBNIOSTIKOS ' means? Look in your dictionaries and see if you can find it there. I learnt to spell that word when I was a little boy, and I used to think it was a wonderful thing to be able to spell a word so big as that with so many letters in it. And when I first heard the *kapua* shouting at a devil ceremony in Ceylon, I was very strongly reminded of my old friend, the longest word that I knew, and I found that what he said meant just as much as that did; that is, nothing but sound.

And the sound in Gregoris Appu's back-yard was increasing every minute. There was not only the shouting of the priest, but the dogs had taken the matter up, as is the way of dogs, and especially Singhalese village dogs. They were determined not to be beaten by the priest in their power of making a noise, so they howled as if they had been resting all day to gather strength for this performance at night. Dogs understand more than we sometimes give them credit for, and they seemed to understand that they could be of some assistance in this noisy ceremony.

The priest was not satisfied with shouting, but, like the 'old lady of Banbury Cross' in the nursery rhyme, he had 'rings on his fingers and bells on his toes;' and as he shouted he danced in the most frantic manner, and the little bells about his feet rang violently. Every now and then he would dance close to poor Marihami's bed and would shout into her mouth to make the demon, supposed to have taken possession of her, take his departure from her and pass into the fowl which was tied to her leg.

Poor Marihami! Could anything be sadder? Can you imagine a more sorrowful

sight in the world than that of this poor
Singhalese mother, stretched out on that mat
on the floor of the verandah, suffering intense
pain and having to endure that cruel ceremony?

There she lies on her hard bed, with a
dim hope that these fantastic rites and wonderful words may relieve her of her pain. If
you, her little white sisters, could only look
at her as she lies there, her thin, pinched
features appearing ghastly in the glare of the
torch; and remember at the same time that
hundreds of these dark-skinned sisters of
ours will to-night be brought out at the
signal of the devil priest's drum to go through
similar cruel ceremonies for the healing of
their diseases, I think you would say, 'They
must have schools. The daughters must not
grow up like that!' And you would do what
you can to prevent the calamity. There she
lies, the poor Singhalese woman, waiting for
you, my sisters, her sisters, to bring her the
brighter hope.

That was not all. At about midnight a
strange procession came into the compound.
It was intended to represent a funeral procession. Four men walked through the
place carrying a bier on which a clay image

was laid. What do you think this was for?
It was in order to try to deceive the evil
spirit. They would make the demon believe
that Marihami was dead and that this was her
dead body which they were carrying away,
and that, therefore, as he had done his worst,
there was no reason why he should not take
his departure! Is it not very sad to think
that people should be so ignorant and wicked
in these days?

Where was Punchi Nona all this time?
In the one bedroom of the house a little girl
with long black hair might be seen kneeling
by the one rough couch of the house. And
her eyes were filled with tears as she prayed:
'O Lord Jesus! come to my poor mother,
who is so ill, and let her touch the hem of
Thy garment, like the sick woman in the
beautiful story in the Bible, that she may be
made whole. And, dear Lord, have mercy
on these wicked people. Show them how
wrong it is to worship devils and trust in the
devil priests, and turn them to Thyself.
Lord, bless dear father and make him, like
the men in the Gospel, a fisher of men for
Jesus Christ. And, dear, good Lord Jesus,
please take care of little Gregoris. He

doesn't know how to take care of himself. Help him to love Thee, Lord, and keep him good. Amen.' The prayer was in Singhalese, but that was very much like what she said when put into English. It will be seen that the Scripture lessons in the school had made a very great impression on her mind, and her teacher had taught her the true nature of prayer to Jesus Christ. She was getting to understand that the Saviour might be near her and would listen to what she said, although she could not see Him.

Baby Gregoris was strutting about the compound in a very impressive manner, trying to make the people believe that he was the most important person in the house. He was the only member of the family who seemed to take any pleasure in the proceedings. Gregoris senior was sitting under the shade of a cocoa-nut palm, looking very thoughtful. He was thinking that it would be a long time before he would have another devil dance, and the probability that Punchi Nona was right and they were wrong dawned upon him more clearly than ever.

Gregoris junior looked at the rice cakes and sweets which had been placed about in

the little booths to satisfy the hunger of any
evil spirits that might be passing that way,
and as he looked he was feeling a strong
temptation to test their power of satisfying his
hunger, when a dog came putting its cold
nose against little Gregoris' leg, as if he had
found a tempting bite too, and Gregoris, in
his hurry to prevent the dog from giving way
to that temptation, turned the booth with all it
contained over upon the ground.    There
were the beautiful rice cakes and the sweets
lying on the sand.    And Gregoris—I am
afraid he was not a very brave boy—began
to cry; he thought he had done something
very dreadful: and while he was crying, the
dog, as is the way of dogs, made good use of
his opportunity, until the priest, attracted by
the sounds of sobbing, arrived on the spot.

The priest's wrath at the accident seemed
to know no bounds.    The evil spirits for
whom the food was intended would cause un-
heard of calamities to descend on poor
Gregoris.    Gregoris senior came to the
rescue, and suggested that it was the dog
who had eaten the sacred cakes, and not
Gregoris, and if anybody suffered for it, it
ought to be the dog.    He would watch that

dog to see if anything happened to it. And the dog did not seem to mind it in the least, but strolled away with a low growl of satisfaction which intimated that he had had a good feed for once in his poor, wretched dog of a life.

Marihami got better. The demon priest claimed the recovery as the result of the ceremony, but Punchi Nona said it was her prayer to the Lord Jesus which had done it, and her father was inclined to agree with her. And Gregoris junior after the accident to the rice cakes always declared in his juvenile way that he didn't care for devil ceremonies. I think he regretted that he had not eaten the cakes.

Now, my dear young friends, you must bear in mind that this degrading, cruel ceremony is not at all uncommon, and nobody knows how many people lose their lives through being brought out to endure all the shocks of the disgusting performance which I have tried to describe. But you will see what our girls' schools save the poor women from, and how they are saved: I think I might almost say that no woman who has been educated in one of our schools would take part in one of these devil ceremonies.

# CHAPTER VII

## THE EXAMINATION.

AS you read the heading of this chapter, it will recall to your minds times of great anxiety and nervous dread not so very long ago. I am assuming, you see, that you are all young people who are reading this little Singhalese village story. And probably, with many of you, examination days are not yet over. O dear me! when I think of my examinations, and the fear and trembling with which I looked forward to them, I wonder that I outlived them. But, like many other things that used to frighten us when we looked forward to them and cause us anxious days and sleepless nights, they do not appear half as big or as dreadful when you look back upon them, unless you fail, and then—well, people do fail sometimes, you know, and if they are the right sort, they try again until they succeed.

Punchi Nona could not sleep a wink the night before the examination. Her mind was entirely occupied with the troubles of the coming day. She lay on her little mat on the floor. That was her bed, and a mat like that is the bed of nearly all the poorer natives of the East. So that, you see, the poor cripple whom our Lord healed would have had no difficulty in doing what he was commanded to do—take up his bed and walk—with such a bed as that. Punchi Nona tossed about on the mat. She was thinking of that great man, the government inspector, who was expected the next day to examine the school. And as she could not sleep, she tried to remember what she had learnt in school. It was not a wise thing to do, because she needed all her strength for the day's work; but she was not so much accustomed to examinations as perhaps you are.

Everybody in Nidigamma was looking out for the inspector that morning. The people felt more than an ordinary interest in him. The school had worked its way into their favour so far as to have in it girls from most of the houses in the place. And then, too, it was not every day that a big English gentleman like the inspector paid them a visit.

The dogs were on the alert, of course,

and seemed to understand that something unusual was going on.

Gregoris Appu senior was in the back verandah, trying to prevail on Punchi Nona to eat a fine, great, fat *hopper* and drink a little coffee. The ' *hopper* ' is an Englishified name for a sort of thick pancake made of very fine rice flour and cocoanut. I think you would like it, most people do. But Punchi Nona did not care for *hoppers* or anything else to eat just then. 'Baby' Gregoris was expecting no examination, and did not hesitate to eat the *hopper*.

Marihami, although she had recovered from her severe illness, was still very unwell, and took but a languid interest in what was going on. But, nevertheless, a great change was taking place in poor Marihami's life. Punchi Nona was becoming a quiet authority in the family. Marihami would raise no opposition to her daughter's suggestions for the improvement of affairs in the house. Cleanliness was beginning to prevail, much to the disgust of 'Baby' Gregoris, who thought it was quite unnecessary to wash himself more than once a week, because he would be sure to get dirty again.

But the little schoolgirl would have her way in such things, and Gregoris Appu had called her in fun on two or three occasions, when he was pleased with her doings in the house, 'Punchi Ammah'—'little mother.'

He would watch her with admiring eyes as he lay on the mat on the floor, after a hard night in the boat, while she busied herself in cleaning the very little furniture they had and brushing away the cobwebs from the walls; and he thought that the house was getting to be a much more comfortable place to live in since the Girls' School was opened in Nidigamma. And there were some pictures on the walls that Gregoris liked to look at. They were pictures from the *British Workman* and *Band of Hope*, which Punchi Nona had had given her in school by the Missionary. His work was chiefly night work, and he would lie for hours on the mat during the day and look at the pictures. And it did him good to look at them. He got disgusted with the horrible pictures painted on the walls of the temple. I do not think people understand how useful good pictures are to those who are engaged in Mission work in the East. Picture language, you know, is a language that everybody can read and understand. I do not mean such picture language as you see on the old monuments in the British Museum. The Hindu and Buddhist priests know how fond people are of being taught in picture language, and so they cover the walls of their temples with that sort of teaching, and very bad teaching theirs is too: very often such as I should not like to show you by any means.

Gregoris was learning a great deal in a quiet way from the pictures on the wall. They taught the virtues of cleanliness. And Gregoris had no difficulty in seeing that the pictures spoke very loudly against the vice of drinking intoxicating liquors, and he very rarely paid a visit to the arrack tavern now. Then—I was going to say over the fireplace, but there are no fireplaces in the houses there; it is hot enough without any thought of a fire, I can tell you—in the place of honour there is a portrait of an ex-President of the Conference, taken out from our big magazine. Gregoris told his friends, when they asked who that gentleman was, that that was the *nayaka unnanse,* the ' high priest ' of the

great *samagama*, or society. And Gregoris
would say it with such an air of importance
that some of his friends would think it had
been sent him by the 'high priest' himself
because of the service he had rendered the
Society in the matter of the school.

But, dear me, how I am wandering! I
always do when I get amongst these Singhalese village characters. I headed this chapter with 'The Examination,' and I have been
all this time writing and saying nothing about
it; and if I do not control my old, gossipy
pen, I shall get through the chapter without
telling you anything about it, and that would
not do, would it? But before I begin to describe the examination I should like to say
·that you might be able to help in the sort of
picture teaching that I have been talking
about. You could send pictures and picture
books. It does not matter if they are a little
soiled—send them to the Ladies' Committee
at the Mission House, and they will be sure
to find their way out to do the good work
which we have seen them doing in the home
of Gregoris Appu.

Now the inspector has arrived, H.M. Inspector of Schools, you know. I think it was

that H.M. that made him so wonderful in the
eyes of Nidigamma.  People think a great
deal of having a lot of mysterious letters before and after their names.   And when Gregoris got to understand from Punchi Nona
that H.M. meant ‘Her Majesty,’ the great
queen, he did not wonder at his daughter’s
nervousness.   It was a great government
man, and who could stand before him without trembling?  Gregoris came out to the
door in a little clean white jacket—a jacket,
by the way, which Punchi Nona had been
taught to make for him in school—and bowed
low as the carriage passed with the wonderful man in it, accompanied by a servant in
the livery of the government.  The people
looked on that servant with as much awe as
you regard a company of life guardsmen, and
probably a great deal more.

Then Gregoris took Punchi Nona by the
hand and hurried after the carriage to the
school.  Young Gregoris, who was always
ready for any bit of excitement, brought up
the rear with a crowd of dogs, who all
thought they would like to be at the examination.  It was quite easy for the dogs to
attend that examination, because there were

no doors to the schoolroom. There were several doorways, but no doors in them. We had not money enough to put in either doors or windows, and so the dogs and crows would often come to school and stand there for a long time looking very thoughtful while the teacher was talking, and would then retire laughing, in dog and crow fashion, at the thought of having had so much education for nothing, and of being allowed to come and go when they like. Even the monkeys in the breadfruit trees seemed interested. We cannot tell what they said about the matter, but it is a fact that they were unusually noisy. Perhaps they were having a school examination of their own, conducted by a big solemn-looking fellow who had swung himself on in the most slow and dignified manner—for a monkey— to the biggest and strongest branch of the tree. Monkeys are such peculiar folk.

The school was beautifully decorated—the teachers had seen to that, and the parents had brought large quantities of moss and ferns and fruits of various kinds, which they tied about the poles on which the roof was supported. On the wall behind the desk, there was a mossy inscription of welcome to Her Majesty's Inspector of Schools. Little Gregoris liked the decorations, especially the fruity part. It made his mouth water to look at it. And he made up his mind to be in the neighbourhood when the decorations were taken down.

The first business was to read the list, and Punchi Nona was the first on that list. And she was in the first group to be examined. Their parents—I think I can see them now— stood at the back of the school and nodded, smiling to each other as the different names were called out. Punchi Nona's voice trembled as she tried to answer the first question. And she knew that she was nervous, and, like many of you under such circumstances, she thought more of what she could not do than of what she could do. The inspector put a very simple, easy question to her, but she felt as if she could not open her mouth. She tried to speak, but the words would not come. Then the tears began to flow. Poor child! she had been so excited with the preparation that her strength had given way entirely in the presence of the great man. There was a pause, during which Gregoris Appu felt like sobbing himself, and began to doubt whether the school was such a blessing to the place as he had thought.

But the inspector knew how to treat such cases. If he had been like some examiners who seem to think that it is their business to get as many failures as possible instead of trying to get the children to show what they really do know, he would have looked very sternly at Punchi Nona, put down a big O opposite her name, and passed on to the next. This inspector knew better. He looked at her very kindly and said in Singhalese: ' You must not cry, my dear. I know that you can answer me very well. You are just a little frightened, that's all. I have a little daughter at home about your age, and she says she is never afraid to be examined by me, because I understand her. Now I think I understand you. Imagine, if you can, that it is your father examining you.'

This made the entire group laugh heartily. The thought of Gregoris Appu taking the place of Her Majesty's Inspector of Schools was too much for them altogether. But it had the desired effect ; it put them all at their ease. The inspector knew what he was about. Punchi Nona passed in every subject. Instead

of the big O there was a X opposite her name
in every column of the big paper in which the
results were entered.   I question if some of
you would have passed a better examination.
And her examiner told her that what she had
learnt she had learnt more thoroughly than
any girl he had met with in the district.   And
she would certainly have failed in every subject
but for the inspector's kind words.   If there
was any chance of this little story going out
to Ceylon, I should say : 'School inspectors,
please copy.'

As soon as the examination was over, the
inspector did what is not usual with inspectors
—he made a little speech, in which he said
some very good things about the school, and
told the parents that if they wanted the
children to live happy and useful lives this
was the way to set about it.   In his speech
he mentioned Punchi Nona and one or two
other girls, and poor old Gregoris Appu's
heart began to throb as violently as if he had
been running a mile uphill without stopping
for breath.

They were all agreeably surprised with the
inspector's speech.   They had thought he was
a great man who would look grand and solemn

and say very little; that, apart from the examination, he would sit in his chair and look like a statue, just as cold and just as hard, and a great deal more unapproachable.

It was a great day for Nidigamma. As the great man was leaving the school, a very intelligent boy in an Englishified dress who had been watching the proceedings with great interest, shouted out the Singhalese for ' *Three cheers for his honour the inspector !* ' It was Ratnaike, who was home from the big town school for his holidays. This shout was followed by another of ' Three cheers for the teacher ! ' Then a young wag cried, ' Three cheers for everybody ! ' which tickled the crowd immensely. And they were still more amused at little Gregoris Appu, who called out in a little piping voice, ' Three cheers for me ! '

Then Gregoris Appu kissed Punchi Nona. Singhalese people do not kiss each other as you do, as I kiss my little nieces for instance, and as they kiss me. The Singhalese kiss is a sniff. They kiss with their noses. I dare say they like it very well, but I must confess that I like our way better.

Gregoris senior kissed his daughter, and

then said, as if he had not been trembling all the time himself:

'What were you so frightened about, my dear? He is nothing but a man, you know, after all.'

'Yes, but I didn't know that till he began to talk like a man, and said I was to think it was you examining me, and I was obliged to laugh.'

And Gregoris laughed heartily as he took her by the hand and led her away from the school. Here they were joined by Ratnaike, who came forward to offer his congratulations. But Gregoris junior had determined to wait to see the decorations taken down, and was there looking with hungry eyes on a big cluster of cocoanuts and plantains hanging on a pole. And I think you would have forgiven him if you could have seen that bunch of fruit.

# CHAPTER VIII.

## CHIEFLY ABOUT GREGORIS APPU JUNIOR.

WE left Gregoris in the last chapter watching the cocoanuts in the decorations. In this chapter we find our poor little friend in a very sad plight indeed. Punchi Nona would not have allowed him to remain behind under ordinary circumstances. He was much too small a child to be allowed to go far by himself. He was quite content, however, to be overlooked on this occasion. His interest in the fruit was so great that it was some time before he discovered that he was alone. Then it struck him that he might have to wait a long time if he waited till the decorations were taken down by the right parties, and he might as well do something in that way himself. You see Gregoris was standing in the way of temptation, and I am sorry to say that he gave way to the temptation. There was no excuse for him, for he knew better; he knew it was wrong, that the nuts were not his.

At first he tried to reach them from the ground. He thought he was very much taller than he really was. Then he thought he would go home and tell Punchi Nona how he had overcome the temptation. Then he heard some monkeys chattering in the trees, and he knew that they would come for the nuts if he were to leave. That was how the poor little rascal argued the matter out to himself and his own satisfaction.

Small as he was, he could climb, and it was not far to climb. So he grasped the pole with his little naked black arms and legs, and in a short time was within reach of the fruit. He had got the biggest nut, and was shaking it to loosen it from the pole, when he heard hurried footsteps coming up the garden. Gregoris in his excitement lost his balance and fell to the ground at the feet of Punchi Nona, who had run back to the schoolroom on discovering that her little brother was not with them.

For some time the poor little fellow lay there like one dead. He had fallen with his back on a log of wood which had been serving the purpose of a form, and his sister saw from the paleness which overspread his face, and

the fact that he did not scream, that he had
received some serious injury. She ran for
assistance, weeping as she went and praying,
'O Jesus, blessed Jesus, bring him to life
again; quickly, Lord Jesus, bring him back
again!' She seemed to think he was dead.
Before they got to the house the little boy
opened his eyes and then said faintly, 'O my
back! I very wicked, sister. O my back!'

How uncertain everything is in this life,
except what relates to the blessed life which
is eternal! Gregoris senior was giving Marihami an account of the examination, and was
telling her what his 'lordship the inspector'
had said about Punchi Nona; and the mother,
usually so indifferent, had become quite interested, and showed her motherly pride in
her face. She had no idea, she said, that a
girl could ever do anything like that. It was
just as she was expressing herself in that way
that a neighbour appeared at the door bearing
his sad burden in his arms. With a scream
she pressed the child to her breast, and he
groaned again, 'O my back! I very wicked
boy. O my back!'

There was weeping and bitter sorrow in
the house of Gregoris Appu. Marihami said

it was all in consequence of the education
Punchi Nona had been getting. If she had
not been carried away by these new-fangled
English notions, she would not have neglected
her little brother. It was an unlucky day, she
knew that from the way the lizards chirped.
The father still contended that Punchi Nona
had been a better sister and a better daughter
ever since she had attended the school. And
little Gregoris would say, as he lay there on
the mat and heard his mother denouncing this
new teaching : ' No, mother dear, not sister's
fault; I very wicked little boy. O my
back ! '

Poor Punchi Nona ! she did nothing but
pray. She thought the Lord had answered
her prayer in bringing her little brother back
to life again when she saw him wake out of
his unconsciousness; and now she prayed that
the Lord would make him quite well. But
that was not to be. The *wedarala* (native
doctor) said that the fall had so injured the
boy's back that he could not possibly recover.
He did not think he could live long, and he
would advise them to call in the demon priest
and arrange for the usual ceremony.

Marihami was inclined to give heed to

the suggestion, but her husband said it should not be. He knew of something better than that. Punchi Nona's prayers were worth scores of devil ceremonies. And little Gregoris agreed with his father. He said: 'I not like debbil dance. I like Punchi Nona pray and sing.' And the sister sang and prayed day after day for nearly a fortnight. Gregoris Appu went to his work and returned with hardly a word to anybody. His neighbours respected his grief and rarely spoke to him. They understood that the greatest sorrow that can come to a Singhalese family was coming to his—the loss of an only son. One of his comrades did say to him one night, as they were in the boat together: 'If it had only been the girl, now, it wouldn't have been so bad, my friend, would it?' 'Yes, it would,' he replied shortly; 'I can ill do without either.' At which unusual sentiment in regard to the comparative value of boy and girl, the other was greatly amazed, and said under his breath to another of the little crew, tapping his head significantly: 'Poor fellow! his troubles are driving him mad.'

The end was coming near. Marihami knew it, and she passed the time in moaning

and groaning, and seemed to take a sort of
comfort out of her sighs.   Poor thing! she
did not know any better.   The father, he sat
in silence looking at the pictures on the wall.
There was one picture in which he seemed to
be especially interested.   You may see it if you
look over your back numbers of the *British
Workman;* it is entitled 'The Good Shepherd,' and it represents Jesus Christ dressed
like an Eastern shepherd with a dear little
lamb in His arms.   If it had not been for
that picture, I think he would have thought
of our Saviour as looking something like a
fine English gentleman.   At first sight he
had understood something of what the picture
meant.   It was one of the last that Punchi
Nona had pasted on the wall.   Little Gregoris
noticed his father's earnest gaze on the picture,
and he soon got as deeply interested in it as
his father.   At last the feeble voice of the
little invalid broke the silence into which they
had fallen.   'I know now who it is—why,
it's the *booful Man* Punchi Nona talked about
that day when  mother was so sick and the
priest came and frightened us with the ugly
face.'   This was brought out in the intervals
of a distressing cough, and Gregoris went on

as well as the cough would let him. 'She said the booful Man had a booful name. He's called Jesus, 'cause He saves.' 'And how do you know it's the same Man, my poor child?' 'How? 'cause He looks so good and booful, and 'cause He's saving that poor little sheep. I know now; Punchi Nona told me all about it one day. Here she comes! Sister, tell father the story of the naughty lamb and the Good Shepherd Who went out into the jungle to search for him.'

Then she got her little Singhalese Testament and read our Saviour's story of the shepherd who left the ninety and nine sheep that were gathered into the fold to go and search for the poor, foolish little sheep who had run away from home. And then she read the touching story of the poor foolish boy who went away from home, to show what the other story meant.

Gregoris the elder was weeping as he had never wept before. The picture teaching was going down into his heart. Little Gregoris was still looking on the 'booful Man' in the picture on the wall

'I see now,' he said; 'me and that poor, silly little lamb are all same. I very

G

naughty boy, I go into jungle. The booful
Man, He come and say: "Poor, stupid little
Singhalese lamb, I leave the fine people in
the great country over the sea and in the
big town, and I come out in jungle for you;
you just get up here." And He put His
arms round me, and I cling to His neck.
Yes; I see, that silly little lamb what lost
hisself and cried *baa-a* in the jungle, his name
Gregoris Appu.'

It was a great effort for the little boy to
say so much. It was said slowly, in Singhalese, of course, but I have given you what
it would be like in English, and it was frequently interrupted with fits of coughing.
The Missionary came just then, and hearing
from the sister what her little brother had
been saying, he proposed that he should be
baptized. The sacrament was explained as
simply as possible to the dying boy, and in
the name of the holy Trinity Gregoris was
received into the visible Church of God.

Yes, the end was drawing near. It was
only a little bit of a life that the child had
lived, and this was the end. It was a beautiful
ending. God was 'perfecting praise out of
the mouths of babes and sucklings,' and the

dying boy was teaching great things to the half-heathen parents. It was surprising to find what a knowledge of Divine truths had been stored in the little fellow's mind in his daily attendance at school, and his talks with Punchi Nona. There he lay on the mat with his back and head propped up. And he looked out through the back door, through a splendid avenue of palms, out upon the great sea, the Indian Ocean. It was the time of the setting sun, and Gregoris, as he looked out between the palms, could see the big shining thing half above and half below the water, with the clouds spread out on either side like angels' wings. The poor, suffering child smiled. It was a grown up sort of a smile, not like that of a child. And he looked a far-off sort of a look, out through the palms, out over the sea, out beyond where the sun was setting. Gregoris the elder saw that he was going, and took him by the hand. The little hand was cold and damp. The little lips moved. Punchi Nona bent her head to hear what he was saying.

'Sister, the booful Man is coming down from the mountain over there, and His face is most glorious. They have put a golden carpet over the great sea for Him to walk on, and He 's coming up under the palms. This way, booful Man, good Shepherd. I the silly little lamb in the jungle. My name Gregoris Appu! This way, come, Lord Jesus!' The Lord came and gathered the poor, silly little Singhalese lamb to His bosom.

# CHAPTER IX.

## PRIZE DAY.

YOU know very well that prize day is like a big school birthday. And like a birthday it only comes once a year, but unlike a birthday it does not come once a year to everybody. Do you remember how little Alice in that strange, wonderful book, *Through the Looking-glass*, enters into a big sum in arithmetic with 'Humpty Dumpty, who sat on the wall,' to show that the year would be ever so much happier if her friends would 'keep up' her 364 un-birthdays and let the birthday go? I have no doubt whatever that scores of little boys and girls are in that state of mind in regard to prize days at school. Of course you know better than to look at things in that way, but I am afraid there are lots of boys and girls who do not.

A rumour had gone through Nidigamma, just as rumours will go through country villages in England sometimes, that is, in the liveliest way imaginable, that a *box* had come

from England for the girls' school, and
rumour, as usual, was busy with the contents
of that box.  The mothers talked of it as
they stood pounding the rice in the big
wooden mortar, making the thud of the heavy
piece of wood on the soft white flour keep up
a sort of rhythmic, or musical, accompaniment
to the stream of gossip.  That is the flour
out of which the *appa cakes* will be made to-
morrow morning, a truly delicious morsel and
a very good thing for beginning the day with
—so the children think ; but when they get
as big and as old as I am, they will think about
what they call their ' digestions ' and resist
the temptation of the cake.

The boy who drives the oxen at the village
cocoanut oil mill and takes care to sit on the
yoke, who looks not unlike our poor little
friend Gregoris—he has heard about the box,
and, after the manner of Singhalese youth, he
extemporises a song about it, which he sings
through his nose to the dog with exceeding
slowness as to time, and with only two notes
in the range of his music.  The dog has come
to see if he can get one of the chips of dried
cocoanut spread out on the ground prepara-
tory to being put in the mill to have the oil

THE VILLAGE OIL MILL.

pressed out of them. He thought the boy would probably be asleep, and is disgusted to find him perched on the beam of the mill droning away like a big bee about a box and a lot of silly girls. It was the dog who had eaten the cakes at the devil ceremony, and had acquired an immense relish for cocoanuts. These dogs have wonderful digestions. Sometimes they look as if they were *nothing but digestion* with nothing to digest.

The box was the theme of conversation too with the 'lords of creation' as they sat or lay on the shore mending their nets. Poor fellows! They did not look much like your idea of lords as they lay about in the scantiest costume, in all sorts of attitudes, lazily stitching the torn meshes; for they will lie if they can at all, and the character of the couch is a matter of very little importance to them.

The fame of the box had even reached the *gansabbawa*, or 'village council.' That is a big name for a big thing. It is a Sanskrit name for a very old institution. It is a company of village elders who act as magistrates, and meet together under a president appointed by the government and govern a village just as those big people the mayor and corporation govern the towns in England. And I think the *gansabbawa* was just as grand to the people of Nidigamma as his worship the mayor and their honours the corporation are to us. In fact, it has much more power in Nidigamma than their worships and their honours have in our English towns. The *gansabbawa* is not only a board of magistrates, but also a board of guardians and a school board as well. It was a general board for settling every village difficulty. You must look at your dictionaries if you do not know what kind of a board I am writing about now.

Well, this board of elders had very little to do on this day, so they looked their wisest looks at the few people who came to see them do nothing, and then the president said he had received an intimation from his honour the Government Agent that he would visit Nidigamma on the occasion of the prize day at the girls' school, and would like to see the village elders at or about that time.

Now a government agent is a great man, a much greater man than his worship the mayor is in England. I am not sure that the right honourable Richard Whittington, thrice lord mayor of London, was a greater man than is a Ceylon government agent in the province which he governs. His influence is unbounded within those limits. Many kings and princes have not half the power that he has over populations that would make a fair little principality.

The poor native farmer looks up with unbounded reverence to this great man, this mighty *dissawe*, or rather he does not look up at all, but bows his head to the ground before him, and is made glad for a lifetime if the prince should give him a kindly word.

Fortunately the prince is generally a man of kindly disposition. He is nearly always a man of experience, and considers himself a 'heaven-born statesman.' He has acquired a wise look, which goes a long way with the Singhalese villager. It is a broad, thoughtful gaze that he gives you, which makes you think that he is making a special study of the subject of conversation, when all the time he is wondering if his cook can be trusted with the fish curry which he ordered before coming into the office to see you.

He is not tyrannical. He is irritable, that is to say, dyspeptic. He does not believe in the activities of life, but is generally passive, except when suffering from a severe attack of dyspepsia or gout. He has got his princely rank through his inactivity, his inability to do harm or create a revolution, accompanied as it is with that thoughtful look which indicates profundities of policy and statecraft undreamt of in any court in the world except the *kach-cheri* over which his highness presides.

And if he would take the trouble to be tyrannical, he knows that it would not pay. There are 'those newspaper fellows:' they have their fingers in everybody's pie, and they sometimes make the plums of princely John Horner taste sour and nasty; and there are 'aboriginal protection societies,' and all sorts of other societies with long names; and there is a House of Commons and a public opinion in England: and altogether it is not worth the prince's while to be tyrannical even if he should feel inclined to be. To do him justice, he does not generally feel so inclined.

He does not dress in a grand uniform, or ride in a gilt coach like my lord mayor: that is a drawback perhaps amongst a people fond of display, but they recognise the old royal look — the 'smile serene and high' — and they do their salaams and sing the prince's praise.

*Griffins, i.e.,* Europeans fresh to the country, who have never seen his highness, talk of him as the 'government agent' with as little reverence as they would talk of an agent for an insurance society; but let them once get the honour of an introduction, and they wonder how they could ever be so irreverent as to apply the term *agent* to so exalted a being. And the princely dignity is maintained.

You will be wanting to know by this time what all this has to do with Punchi Nona and the Nidigamma school. It has this to do with it: I wanted you to understand how great an honour was being put on the school in this contemplated visit of the great government man, and so I thought I would try to describe him, and in doing so I have fallen into a style of writing not well adapted for youngsters like you, but which I cannot help if I take the pen in some of my moods. The printer can leave that part out if he likes, or if he lets it stay you can skip it.

You will understand then that the government agent is a very great man indeed; and

the agent of whom I speak was not only a
man of great influence, but he was a good
man, and knew how to use his influence for
good, as you will find when we come to
read his little speech at the prize-giving.
You will find, if you look at our Reports, that
several of these gentlemen give largely towards the support of our schools; and this
we take as a very good proof, coming as it
does from men of great experience of work
amongst the natives, that they consider it the
truest statesmanship to encourage the spread
of Missionary education.

When it was known in Nidigamma that
the honourable the government agent had
written to the Missionary, saying that it
would give him very great pleasure to take
part in the distribution of the prizes that had
come in the wonderful box, the people, high
and low, gave the school that attention which
people generally do give, even in civilized
countries like England, to affairs that are
'under distinguished patronage.'

The mysterious box all this time was at
the Mission house, some distance away. It
was not such a mystery to the Missionary
and his wife, because they had opened it.

And besides they had received a list of the contents from the secretary of the Ladies' Committee, stating what kind friend had given this, and who had given that, and what little girl had worked a dress for the doll prize. I should not be surprised to find that some of your names have been down on similar lists. I hope so.

I wish you could have seen the opening of that box and heard what was said during the ceremony; why, it would have done you as much good as a juvenile Missionary meeting and a great deal more good than some big, grown up Missionary meetings that I have been at.

They make quite a little ceremony of it in an informal sort of a way. The Missionary comes in with his hammer and chisel into the box-room and looks as solemn as if he were about to lay the foundation stone of a chapel or something of that kind. The wife scarcely waits for the cover to come off before she grasps a doll and holds it up to the admiration of the family group. There are two or three dolls with waxen constitutions who cannot stand the tropics. But with the exception of the two or three sickly little ladies, everything is beautiful.

Then the things are arranged according to the list from the Ladies' Committee. The prizes are separated from the things to be sold, and the lady calculates how much the things will make. And the Missionary wonders whether a bazaar could not be held in the chief town of the province, where there are some Europeans to buy and where the Government Agent lives. It would be a poor little affair, but it would be something towards an idea that he has had in his mind for some time—that of building a nice little school chapel which would be more attractive and comfortable for the people than the present mud schoolhouse. Then a bright idea strikes Mrs. Missionary, and a note is dispatched to Mrs. Government Agent to ask her to come to the prize giving, in order to enlist her sympathies for the bazaar. You see I am letting you into all sorts of secrets and showing you how the little details are managed sometimes.

But really we must stop this yarning about the box and get to the prize day. Nidigamma never looked so gay as it did on the morning of that day. It did not deserve its name one bit that day. Have I ever

told you what the name means? It means
'the sleep village.' There are many villages
in Ceylon that the name would fit; but there
is a story about the giving of the name to
this village. The story is that an Indian
prince was expected to pass through, and as
he did not reach the village in the daytime,
as was expected, but somewhere near midnight when all honest folk are abed, the good
people of Nidigamma didn't hear, or couldn't
hear, the cries of the heralds who proclaimed
the coming of the prince, and wouldn't stir
an inch to see the grand torchlight procession. I cannot say that I blame them very
much, do you? Well, the prince, who was a
very good wit for a prince, suggested that
the village should be called from that time
Nidigamma, or ' the sleep village.'

But Nidigamma was wide awake on the
great day of the prize giving and the coming
of the prince of the new order, the Government Agent. And if the prince had come in
the middle of the night, he would have found
some of the people awake. Punchi Nona was
awake for one. She was anxious for the
sake of her father and mother. Baby Gregoris was gone, and Marihami was getting to

H

understand that a girl might be of as much use in the world as a boy. She had made up her mind to go to the prize giving. Punchi Nona was amazed to see her mother an hour before the time announced for the great event come out of her own little bedroom dressed more grandly than she had ever dressed for a *pinkama,* or to carry an offering to the temple. She had put on all her jewels; they were not many, but with the exception of the little house and garden and the boat they formed all the wealth of the family. It is usual for the Singhalese people to turn their money into jewellery because they can keep it more safely in that way.

Gregoris too had got on his 'Sunday best,' and had put on a beautiful new tortoiseshell comb over his hair, which was getting a little grey.

'O!' he said, as they were walking to the schoolhouse; 'if poor Gregoris were here, he would enjoy this, and no mistake.'

The decorations on the day of the examination and of Gregoris' fall were nothing to the decorations of the prize day. A big platform was erected for the agent and the table on which the prizes were to be laid.

MARIHAMI DRESSED FOR THE PRIZE-GIVING.

H 2

And now there is a whisper, 'Here they come!' and a lane is made, and the Agent and Mrs. Agent and the Missionary friends come and take their places by the platform. Gregoris Appu's little family group is accommodated with seats near the platform too, partly because of the manner in which Gregoris had been identified with the school, and partly because he was there in good time.

The proceedings began with an address to his honour the agent. Ratnaike, the clever boy who had been to the English school in the big town, had learnt that it was the proper thing to read an address when any great man visited a place; and as he was considered the best English scholar in the village, he was asked to write the address. This was the address :—

'To the Honourable the Government Agent of the South Western Province of Ceylon, the adjacent Islands, and the Dependencies thereof, greeting :

'*Mostly honoured master, your honour's petitioners beg to present themselves humbly before your honour's bountiful person to ask mercifully accept our gratitudes and respects for*

your honourable visit.. *We, the people of Nidigamma, beg to assume that we consider it re-
flected a heavy balance to the credit side of
your noble self and also the high and mighty
lady who is to you as a better half, the many
and varied interests which you both have ap-
prehended in the educations of the adolescent
portion of the inhabitants of this sequestrated
commune.* Under your honour's favourable
auspices we intensely believe that the present
seminary for the fair damsels of the district
will increase in glory like the sun in firmament
grandeur, casting overboard the chains of
ignorance and bombarding the castles of superstition, trampling antiquarian prejudices under
foot and gathering under its comforting shade
all the feminine genders of this ancient and
rising populations. And that your honour and
honour's lady may be there to see is the humble
petition of, signed by twenty of the leading
inhabitants of Nidigamma.'*

Besides the Europeans present there were
only three who could understand English, and
they had not studied English composition to
any good purpose, as you may imagine from
the specimen given above.

Ratnaike, like most boys in the early stages
of English education, was under the delusion
that similarity in spelling indicates similarity
in meaning, and, like most such students, he
revelled in figures of speech.   Such addresses
are not at all unusual, and the people will use
English if they can at all on official occasions.

The majority of the congregation thought
it a splendid specimen of the ripest English
scholarship.   Ratnaike was proud of it.   It
showed an acquaintance with all kinds of
literature.   It was a judicious mixture.   And
Punchi Nona was proud of Ratnaike, proud
to think that it was done by a friend of their
family.   Gregoris Appu lifted his head and
gave a great 'what-do-you-think-of-that?'
nod to the company in general.

It seemed to give them a little satisfaction
too to see that the English ladies and gentlemen present were hiding their heads as if in
self-abasement, and were evidently labouring
under great emotion at being beaten in English
composition by the clever youth of the
village.

His honour, the Agent, was so overcome by
the address that it was some time before he
could reply, and when he did, it was in the

briefest manner just to thank them for the remarkable address, saying that he would reserve what he had to say till the prizes were delivered.

A hymn was then sung and prayer offered —in Singhalese, of course. Then the Missionary said a few words and Mrs. Agent gave the prizes.

'First Prize for Good Conduct and General Proficiency—PUNCHI NONA.'

What a tremendous clapping there was to be sure, led off by Ratnaike, who had picked up all sorts of English habits at the big boys' school in the town! And Punchi Nona went slowly and shily up to the platform, looking up through her long, dark eyelashes at the kind lady who was holding out the prize. It was what I believe is called a 'lady's companion'—a sort of portfolio fitted up with scissors, thimbles, needles, hooks and crooks, and a host of other things that had come out in the mysterious box. The lady said she was delighted to hear of what Punchi Nona had been able to do in the school. She hoped she would use the beautiful present which had been sent by the kind ladies in England to the best purpose—that of assisting the work of

clothing the household.    Punchi Nona curt-
seyed as nice a little curtsey as any of you can
make, and came back to place the handsome
present in the hands of her proud mother.

Now, having told you about the first prize,
you know how the others would be given, and
the clapping that would take place, and the
tremulousness of the children, and the smiles
and nods of the parents when their children's
names were announced.    You know all about
it, of course.

After the prizes were distributed his honour
the Government Agent stood up and said,
'My friends,—When our good friend the
Missionary sent me the invitation to be present
to-day, I felt that I could not refuse, although
I had important work in hand which I could
ill afford to neglect.    But I am one of those
who think that no work in such a country as
this is more important than the education of
the young, and especially female education.'
('Hear, hear,' from the middle of the crowd
in the voice of Ratnaike.)    'I will tell you why.
Because any reform, any good work, either in
Church or state, to be lasting must begin at
home—that is, in the homes of the people.
And you know as well as I do that the women

have the greatest influence in the domestic life. A good wife and mother makes a good family and a comfortable home. And good families will make good communities or " communes " as the address calls them. And it is the object of such institutions as these to make your daughters intelligent, respectable, and good, who will bring a new and better life into your homes. I have been exceedingly gratified to learn from my assistants who were here at the last paddy-renting that the improvement in the village since the school was established has been most marked.' ('True! true! I believe it,' said in Singhalese in low voices at the back of the crowd.)

'I hear that there was some opposition when the school was first started, and that it would not have been begun when it was if it had not been for one of your number who had the sense to see how much it was needed. I refer to Gregoris Appu.' (Here Gregoris Appu held his nose in his hand and gave a little, short, deprecating cough.) 'Now I want to ask you whether you are willing to see this school given up after all that it has done for you?' ('*Appooyi,*' 'O my! No, indeed!' shouted from all quarters.) 'Well then, you must do something towards supporting it yourselves. Suppose you find a half of the money, I will then give as much as you raise; and the kind English ladies will be able to use the money for some other village where the people do not see the need of education as you do; and I know a place of that kind not very far from here that I should like to suggest to them.

'I have said nothing about that higher education of the heart which is necessary above all things. Our friend the Missionary will talk to you about that. And for my own part I do not believe much in schools where that education does not come first. Now, in conclusion, I wish the Nidigamma Girls' School all success. I trust and believe that the education given in it will be good and practical, and be of still greater benefit to the village than it has been in the past. I hope also that the day is not far distant when you will have a substantial stone school chapel, and, again quoting the address, "may I be here to see."'

Then of course the clapping was furious. And the meeting was closed with the singing of 'God save the Queen' in Singhalese and the benediction.

At the close of the proceedings Punchi Nona was introduced to Mrs. Agent, and was patted on the head by the great man himself; and you can fancy what a flutter of excitement the little party were in as they walked back from the school-room to the house of Gregoris Appu.

The father was a proud man that day; but there was sadness mingled with the joy, as there is with most of our pleasures. 'I dare say Gregoris is better where he is; but wouldn't the poor little chap have jumped for joy to see this fine what-d'ye call-'em and to hear the great man mention my name!'

Marihami, who was behind, having a bit of gossip with a neighbour, said, 'Well, I should never have dreamt that it was in them; but I declare girls are *nearly* as good as boys.'

Sarnalis, the demon priest, who had overtaken the party, accompanied by his son, Kalu Appu, protested that it made him angry to hear people talking such nonsense. He thought Marihami had got more sense. It was against all reason and all religion. And

it was a sin for which they would suffer
heavily in a future birth, this education of
girls. Sarnalis was not invited into the house
of Gregoris Appu that day. Ratnaike was.
The influence of the demon-priest was on the
decline in Nidigamma.

# CHAPTER X.

## PUNCHI NONA SEES SOMETHING OF THE

## BIG WORLD.

THAT something was not by any means extraordinary. You would think it very little indeed, but to our young friend it was the most remarkable event of her life. No young English lady ever went to her first ' drawing-room ' or ' came out ' in society with more mingled feelings of nervous dread and bewilderment than did Punchi Nona experience in making her first acquaintance with the big world of Ceylon.

In some of your atlases Ceylon looks like a little daub of paint splashed by the brush of the painter in painting the south of India. But it is really a very important country, though the atlases and geographies often ignore it or pass its importance over in the lightest way imaginable. I used to begin some of my deputation speeches in England about Ceylon with a short lesson in geography. I used to say, ' Ceylon is an island nearly as big as Ireland. It is a great deal greener than the Emerald Isle, and, just now, is a much quieter place to live in.' And one who has seen Ceylon has seen a great deal of the big world. It is a central place, and a sort of half-way house for the nations of the earth. East and west are represented there, and sometimes in the course of an hour or so in one of the large towns you may hear twenty different languages spoken.

In Nidigamma these things are talked about, but few have realised them. Ratnaike in his holidays has been accustomed to gather an admiring crowd around him to listen to his stories of 'city life,' as he calls his school experiences; or a Moorman, a Mohammedan pedlar, will come with a big tin box and open it at Gregoris Appu's door. He spreads out all sorts of beautiful cloths, which he says are all that he has left—all the rest, an immense quantity, of course, has been bought by her ladyship, the Government Agent's wife; and he has heard that the Queen of England sent to keep the ships that the cloths came out in : she wanted them all for herself, but she was too late—the ships had sailed; and so Ceylon in general and Nidigamma in particular got

the benefit of it. Then he produces tin trays
from the box with wonderful ribbons, combs,
bottles of perfume, soaps, boxes of pens, ink

THE TAMBY.

bottles, and hosts of other things which I cannot remember now. And when he has spread
his stores out in the big cloth which he keeps

for that purpose, he rises to his full length; for the Moor, or 'Tamby,' as he is called there, is generally a tall, big, strong-looking man. He is a strict Mohammedan, and therefore a strict teetotaller, and that is perhaps one reason why he looks so healthy and strong. He places a peculiar hat on his shaved head, and inquires whether Gregoris Appu's family or any of the neighbours who are crowding around have ever before seen such a sight as that box can show. During the exhibition he gives his audience some news from the cities and towns through which he has journeyed.

You can imagine, therefore, that Nidigamma folk live and die without a very accurate knowledge of the outside world. I do not think they care to know much. Their village is a world big enough for them, so they say. But the school was modifying public opinion in this respect even in Nidigamma.

It was some time after the event described in the last chapter. The school had gone on prosperously. A bazaar had been held. The new school chapel had been built, and built chiefly through the exertions of Gregoris Appu, who spent all his spare time in

promoting the work, and laboured himself in
the building. This labour of love was mentioned to the Government Agent, who thought
the services rendered to education by this
good man deserved some recognition on the
part of the authorities, and so he mentioned
Gregoris Appu to his Excellency the Governor
for a *Muhandiramship.* That is a big word
which I am afraid you will not find in your
dictionaries. *Muhandiram* is a Singhalese
title of rank given to certain native officials,
or conferred by the Government on men who
have distinguished themselves by works of
public usefulness.

The Agent, in writing to the Governor,
intimated that he thought a man who had
built a schoolhouse was as worthy of the
rank as a man who had built a bridge. The
fact of Gregoris Appu being a man of com-
paratively low caste, he hoped, would be no
hindrance, nor the fact that the services
rendered had been given to a school belong-
ing to a dissenting Christian denomination.
Seeing that the Missionary Societies were
aiding the Government in their educational
work and lightening the burden of educational expenditure, he thought that the

Government ought to be more ready to recognise help afforded in that way than even
the regularly paid labours of their own
servants.

Not many Government Agents have had
the courage or the liberal-mindedness to write
letters of that sort to the Governor, and few
Governors, unfortunately, would have granted
such petitions.   But the Governor who ruled
in Ceylon at this time was a worthy representative of good Queen Victoria.   God bless
her !   He was not slow to recognise a good
work anywhere when his attention was called
to it.   In his journeys through the country
he made a point of seeing the schools, especially the girls' schools, and encouraging the
teachers in their good work with kind words
and sometimes with handsome contributions :
so that His Excellency—that is the title
given to Governors, you know—was of the
same opinion as the Government Agent as to
the value of Gregoris Appu's services.

All this will help to explain the sensation
caused in our friend's house one morning
early in April, 18—: well, it doesn't matter
much about the precise date.

A letter was a great event in most of the

houses in Nidigamma, and on this morning a letter was brought to the house of Gregoris Appu. And this was no ordinary-looking letter. It had no postage stamp on it, but there was a sort of stamp at the back, with the old picture of the 'lion and the unicorn fighting for the crown.' Gregoris seemed rather afraid of the letter, and passed it un-opened to Punchi Nona, who read out the grand words, 'ON HER MAJESTY'S SERVICE,' which made poor Gregoris Appu more ner-vous than ever. Then Punchi Nona cour-ageously opened the letter and translated the Agent's brief epistle, which was to the effect that his Excellency the Governor had signified his intention of conferring the title and honour of *Muhandiram* on Gregoris at the next Queen's birthday *levée* in Kandy, of which he would receive further notice.

To say that our friends were surprised would be a weak way of describing the ex-citement of the occasion. Punchi Nona flung her arms round her father's neck and kissed him in the Singhalese fashion. Marihami opened her big, dark eyes wider than usual and began to think of the impression it would make on her friends in the village. Gregoris

Appu rubbed his eyes, then combed his hair,
and asked Punchi Nona to read the letter again.

After the excitement had gone down a
little the question arose as to how they were
to get to Kandy for the investment. Marihami offered to sell some of her jewels, and
Gregoris thought he could sell a share of the
boat. Then it occurred to Marihami that a
friend and relative of hers in Kandy would be
glad to hear of the honour which was to be put
on the family, and as he was well off he might
be disposed to entertain them while there.

So the friend was written to, and as
Gregoris could not go without Marihami,
and it would not do to leave Punchi Nona
at home by herself, they decided that they
would all go together. We must not dwell
on the details of the arrangements for the
journey or on the sensation which it caused
in Nidigamma. It was more than a 'nine
days' wonder.' It lasted for a month, and
increased as the time for the departure drew
near.

Marihami, I regret to say, went in secret
to the village astrologer, who gave her a long
list of signs that would be lucky, and things
that would be unlucky, if seen in the course

of their journey. And he fixed on the luckiest day he could find for starting on. The school had done a great deal indirectly for Marihami, but she still clung to some of her old superstitious practices.

BULLOCK CART.

You will not need to be told that the night previous to the great journey was a sleepless night in the house of Gregoris Appu. Long before it was day a bullock cart was brought to the door to take the family party away.

Two great patient oxen stood there, with the yoke of the cart resting on their necks. They had been lent for the occasion by the road overseer. Beautiful great creatures are these same oxen, calm and submissive, notwithstanding all their wonderful strength.

Punchi Nona looked bright and beautiful as she got into the cart, only it must be confessed that she did it rather awkwardly. Her *comboy*, or skirt, was bound so tightly about her that she found mounting the step to the cart a matter of some difficulty. Both she and Marihami had to be assisted by Gregoris Appu's stronger arm. But I have seen young ladies quite as awkward in England. Three years ago I saw two grown-up young ladies, in England, lifted into an omnibus for the same reason which made it necessary for Gregoris to help his wife and daughter into the bullock cart.

Now they are in their cart and have said 'good bye' to a crowd of friends, amongst whom were Sarnalis and his son, and Ratnaike. Sarnalis had brought Marihami a charm for the journey, a polished piece of bone which she was to tie on her arm to keep the demons away.   Gregoris said it was all ‘ stuff and nonsense.’   Ratnaike was the most important person there, next to the travellers themselves, because he had frequently done the journey as far as Colombo.   And on the strength of this he put on all the airs of a ‘ city man,’ and coached up Gregoris in the mysteries of city. life.

Now the big patient oxen have been wakened out of their reveries about the delicious Guinea grass which they expect when the journey is over.   And with a shout of ‘ *Ja! Ja! Pita! Pita!* ’—which is Singhalese for the ‘ *Gee!* ’ ‘ *Whoa!* ’ which you will hear sometimes in English villages, the cart rattles on with the family party.

On through a great avenue of palms they go, on a road which looks not unlike a stately cathedral aisle, getting glimpses of the wide blue sea through the green arches on the one side, and of the blue peaks of the distant mountains on the other.   Here and there they pass a paddy field with the green heads of the rice grass just appearing above the water.

‘ *Ja! Ja! Pita! Pita!* ’   On, ungracefully but gallantly, the big, patient oxen run.   It is early morning, the sun has not yet climbed

to the top of the highest hills.    There is
Adam's Peak, a very picture of a mountain, and
regarded by millions of people as one of the
most sacred spots in the world.    The peak
itself, rising above the morning clouds, looks
like an immense, pointed blue sapphire resting
on a bed of wool.

'O how beautiful the world is!' shouted
Punchi Nona, as she put her head out over the
curtain of the cart to have a drink of the cool,
clear morning air, and saw the meadowy rice-
fields stretching away to the swelling hills.
'And there is the Peak clearer than I've ever
seen it before in this monsoon.'

'O how fortunate!' said Marihami; 'so
it is : it is the holy hill, the mountain of the
sacred footprint of the lord Buddha!    Did you
see it over your right shoulder?    Well, this is
a lucky day, and the astrologer was right—I
mean, we were right in starting to-day.'

'*Ja! Ja! Pita! Pita!*' The great oxen have
become meditative and need rousing.    It is
not unusual for them to become meditative in
the middle of a journey.    A far-off look gets
into their dreamy eyes.    It is possible that
they love the great, beautiful world and drink
in the morning glory as well as Punchi Nona,

only they cannot talk about it as she can. Who
knows? My private opinion is that often
they are only ' 'tending,' as children say, and
that thoughtful look which you think means
poetry only means the *poonac* (a sort of gruel)
which they expect for breakfast. Association
with men makes one sceptical of beasts.

'*Ja! Ja! Pita! Pita!*' Dear me! we
must get on faster. My gossipy old pen finds
it hard to keep within bounds when it gets on
these subjects. On goes the family of Gregoris
Appu. The monkeys come down from their
leafy shelter in the tops of the trees to have a
good look at the travellers. They swing themselves by their long arms from the branches
and pretend that they are going to jump on
the thatched roof of the bullock cart. I wish
I could stay to tell you some of my monkey
stories, but I cannot. '*Ja! Ja! Pita! Pita!*'
Now we leave the monkeys behind, perhaps
laughing at the slow, heavy, cumbersome way
in which Gregoris travels, compared with their
light, free and easy methods. Now the cart
draws near to a village. There is the village
temple, the *dagoba,* a bell-shaped building
which is supposed to contain some precious
relics; and there close by is the monastery

where, Marihami says, a holy priest lives with
many Buddhist monks.    And now we come
to the low huts thatched with palm leaves,
many of them dirty little shops where women,
who look as if they had slept on the ground,
and 'slept in their hair,' sit on dirty benches
selling rice cakes.    That plain, whitewashed
building on the left is a Methodist chapel.

VILLAGE TEMPLE.

'*Ja! Ja! Pita! Pita!*'    On goes our little
party through village after village, amid the
howling of dogs, the cawing of the crows, and
the shouts of the naked boys who run behind

the cart. The world is awake now, and no mistake. 'The longest lane has a turning,' and this long journey turns at last into Colombo, the capital of the island of Ceylon.

It is impossible for me in the limits of these chapters to tell you all about the wonderful sights which made Punchi Nona say the Singhalese for ' O my ! ' a hundred times that day; of the great buildings and the big ships, the sight of which made Gregoris Appu rub his eyes to be sure that he was not dreaming.

A tall, British soldier in scarlet uniform, whom Gregoris thought to be one of Her Majesty's judges at least, called out as they passed, ' I say, old fellow, could you give us a lift to the station ? ' Gregoris, of course, had no idea that it was not the most elegant English, and told the driver that he thought his lordship very affable. The driver smiled, shook his head, and shouted : '*Ja ! Ja ! Pita ! Pita !* '

On they go through the crowded streets, out by the lake on which the lotus, the lovely massive water lily, floats, and where the *dhoby*, or native washerman, beats the dirt, and, too often, the threads, out of the European linen.

Now the bullocks are made to pull up, and they pretend, as they do it, that they would not mind going miles farther; for this building in front, which you would call 'dumpy,' but which Gregoris thinks a palace, is the railway station, and here a very different journey from the 'bullock drive' begins, but that must hold over for the next chapter.

# CHAPTER XI.

## THE MOUNTAIN CAPITAL.

CAN you remember when you first saw a steam engine? I can. I was small, only just beginning to read the *Juvenile Offering*, when I was taken to see the opening of a new railway near the place where I lived. I remember how we boys clapped our hands and hurrahed as we saw the wonderful iron horse come puffing into the station as if it had been running a race and were panting for breath. No fairy tale ever astonished me so much as that wonderful horse did.

Punchi Nona had read in the school Reader about the 'smoke-carriage,' as the Singhalese people call the locomotive engine. And Gregoris Appu had heard about 'the snorting demon' that the English people had brought into Ceylon. But the stories told in Nidigamma, coloured as they had been, were not equal to what the little party saw as they stood on the platform of the Colombo railway station staring at the engine which came in to take the train to Kandy. There they stood in open-mouthed wonder for some minutes. Even Punchi Nona, who had learnt so much in the English school, looked at it with as much amazement as did her father and mother.

You have probably read the story of 'Sinbad the Sailor' in the *Arabian Nights.* Capital story, is it not? He was an old sailor, and, of course, he had some wonderful yarns. And one of his yarns is about the island of Ceylon. In that story he tells you how he managed to get over a range of high mountains. He tied himself to the leg of a big bird, who flapped his great wings and carried him over the mountains into the country of the king of Serendib, which was the Arabian name for Ceylon.

My private opinion is that that story was a little overdrawn. But we must be careful not to say a thing is overdrawn or untrue because we have never seen it. But what would the sultan to whom the stories in the *Arabian Nights* were told, what would he have said if Scheherazade had made Sinbad describe himself as having been taken to Kandy by the iron horse instead of by the wonderful bird ? I think he would have said it was carrying the thing too far, even for *Arabian Nights*, and he would probably have ordered in the executioner to chop off her head.

Our little party made a great many mistakes on the platform. They were very much confused. At first Gregoris Appu wanted to get on the engine. Then, in their confusion, the whole party bolted madly into a first-class carriage, where they were asked to show their tickets. Their tickets they had neglected to purchase, and it was some time before they could be made to understand that necessary preliminary to the journey.

Their tin boxes were bundled out of the first-class carriage, and Gregoris, after falling over a heap of luggage, might be seen at the ticket-window cautiously untying a knot in the corner of his handkerchief and taking out the money for the fares.

They were helped into a third-class carriage by a guard. There Gregoris found himself—as one may easily find himself, travelling on a Ceylon railway—sitting next a Buddhist priest, opposite a Brahmin, who was chatting most familiarly with a Mohammedan. These railways do a wonderful work in breaking down caste distinctions and bringing people together. While he was thinking of this, a shrill scream of a whistle came from the engine, then a snort. This was followed by a bump of the carriage which brought Gregoris and the Brahmin into very familiar contact indeed, and our friends from the country were fairly started on their journey to Kandy.

'Look! look!' said Marihami, 'why, it's all moving! Look, Punchi Nona! Did you ever see anything like that? The trees are flying! Isn't it wonderful?'

'Yes, mother; but I knew it was going to be like this. It is explained in a book that we read from in school.'

At which reply, which you would perhaps call 'priggish' if a boy had said it, Marihami looked a little cross and said, 'O yes; I dare say. You learn everything at that school, don't you? Perhaps you can tell me what those wires are for.'

Punchi Nona's education had not yet reached to the electric telegraph, and so the explanation was not forthcoming; at which her mother seemed not a little pleased. The Buddhist priest, however, saw the difficulty and volunteered an answer.

'The wires are for *yakhoo* (demons) to walk on. They carry messages faster than the smoke-carriage will.'

'*Appooyi*, my lord! what wonderful people these English are!'

Now they stop at a station called Kalani, where the priest gathers his yellow robe about him, says '*Ayuboon*' ('long life to you') to the little party, and gets out of the carriage; for he is the head of a monastery connected with a celebrated old temple close by.

The carriage is besieged by a group of dirty, naked boys with fruit to sell. One opens a young cocoanut with a big dirty knife, and Gregoris takes a refreshing draught of the delicious milk which it contains. Marihami invests a halfpenny in a pineapple, a juicier one than you would get here for five shillings. Only fancy that! Would you not like to go to Ceylon?

Punchi Nona unties her handkerchief and spends a penny on two mangoes. The mere mention of the mango calls up such delicious memories, and somehow the memories all seem to get into one's mouth! No pen can do the mango justice, and I am sure that mine cannot.

K

The engine whistles and snorts, the carriage bumps, and the train starts again. On they dash over rivers, where alligators quietly float on the water; through thick jungle, where the birds scream and fly as if they had never heard the engine before—they go through that farce every day; out into the paddyfields, where the storks gather their long legs up under their wings and fly away to more restful scenes, to come back again and be frightened in the same way to-morrow.

The big, lazy buffalo knows better. He lifts his head from the mud in which his body is buried and says in the grunting buffalo language, 'It's you, is it? Well, you don't frighten me!' and goes to sleep again till the next train passes.

Now they come to the foot of the mountain range behind which Kandy lies. Here they are joined by two other engines which come to help their brother up the hill. Up the side of the mountain they go, passing waterfalls where the water comes dashing down over a high rock, as if it were going to fall on the carriage, but breaks up at a respectful distance into a beautiful mist, like a fine gauze veil on which the sun lays bands of brilliant colours.

Up and up they go. And the train seems to Gregoris Appu like Rahu, the great dragon of the Buddhist stories, creeping around the mountain. Six miles an hour is not rapid for

THE RICE FIELDS.

a railway journey, but the three engines are panting as if they find it hard work to do it. Now they leave the forests of cocoanut palms behind them, and a great variety of trees with splendid foliage comes into view. The

K 2

tall areca palm is still with them, graceful
and stately, the queen of palms.   O that
wonderful valley down into which our travellers looked from the ascending train!
They said, 'Oh—h!' long drawn out.
And that is just what most travellers say
when they look down into that valley for the
first time.   The hillsides are terraced with
paddy fields, and the whole valley looks like
a mighty colosseum with its galleries draped in
living green, and here and there a fleecy curtain
of cloud.   In one  of the upper galleries
commanding the entire valley stood the
gigantic talipot, the emperor of palms,
clothed with immense leaves, and crowned
with an imperial crown of flower, such as is
rarely seen, even in tropical forests.

Up the engines go, and the travellers
shudder as they look out of the window and
find themselves looking down precipices which
maintain the perpendicular for hundreds of feet
down.   Now they find themselves passing
through thick jungle again, and then through
large coffee estates, where charred and black-
ened stumps of trees relieve the monotony of
the coffee laurel, but do not add to the beauty
of the scenery.

They come to the last stage of the journey, and the views on either side are perfectly enchanting. They pass Peradeniya, with the Royal Botanic Gardens, said to be the finest gardens of the kind in the world.

A PEEP FROM THE ROAD.

There are delightful momentary peeps, between the tall feathery bamboos, of the great river of Ceylon, the Mahawelli Ganga: and in one of these peeps they see the river spanned by a bridge with a beautiful arch; and the bridge is made entirely of satin wood, the most beautiful wood of the Ceylon forest. All these sights are pointed out to our little party as the train dashes into Kandy, the mountain capital of Ceylon.

But Gregoris' party is not deeply interested now in these wayside views; partly because they are tired of fine scenery, and partly because their eyes are smarting with the sparks from the engine, which they have caught in them, and have tried to rub out, and partly because Marihami is not quite sure that they have got all the parcels and tin boxes they started with.

And here is Kandy at last (*see frontispiece*), the royal city of the Lion race, nestling in the valley by the side of its beautiful lake. A friend of mine the other day called it ‘the capital of fairyland.’ There are but few lovelier spots in the world than this same Kandy.

At the railway station they are met by their relatives, and taken home in a bullock cart through the town to the little village outside Kandy, where their friends live. The Kandy friends took a great delight in pointing out the objects of interest as they passed. At a short distance from the station they came to a place where, the Kandy friend said, a dreadful massacre had occurred, early in the present century. The wife of the prime minister had been compelled to perform the office of executioner to her own children at the command, and in the presence of, the cruel Wikrama Singha, the last of the Kandyan kings. 'Then,' he went on to say, 'she drew herself up, and saying, " I am the daughter of a king, and can die bravely with my children ! " she threw herself down into the depths of the lake near which the executions had taken place.'

' What a grand Christian she would have made ! ' said Punchi Nona.

' Ah, there are are no women like that now,' responded the Kandyan, who was one of the sort that are always sighing for ' the good old times.' Kandy never had such ' good times ' as it has to-day under British rule.

I cannot stay to tell you of all the interesting sights they saw during the time that they stayed in this beautiful neighbourhood. They saw the Maligawa, the famous Buddhist temple, one of the most famous in the world. Kandy is very sacred ground

in the Buddhist world.   Our little party saw
one evening, when the gun from the great
tower had announced that the sacred shrine
was open to the view of worshippers, crowds
of pilgrims entering the huge gateway, pilgrims of many nationalities, Chinese, Japanese,
Siamese, **and** Burmese, and some from far-
away Cambodia.

'Wouldn't it be grand, father,' said Punchi
Nona, as she watched them carrying in their
offerings of flowers; 'wouldn't it be grand
if they could learn something about Jesus
while they are here, and go back to talk
about Him to their countrymen?'

Marihami, in whom, I am afraid, the old
heathen leaven was still working, said she
would like very well to join them, and take
flowers to the shrine of the tooth of the holy
Buddha.

'Are all these people going to worship a
tooth?' said Punchi Nona.

'Yes,' replied the Kandyan, who had
accompanied them; 'but it is not a human
tooth at all.   A friend of mine, a Singhalese
gentleman, had possession of it for one night,
during the rebellion, and he took the opportunity to examine it, and he says he has no

THE MALIGAWA, TEMPLE OF THE TOOTH.

doubt whatever that it is the tooth of an
alligator ! '

'And yet it is that " false tooth " which
makes Kandy so sacred in the eyes of so
many millions of people ; and there it is inside
that temple, covered with shrines of gold,
over which a network of jewellery is hung,
big sapphires, rubies, and cats' eyes that would
make a ransom for a king.'

The little party stood for some time on
the broad green where the Kandyans were
accustomed—in 'the good old times,' as
Gregoris reminded his friend—to fall on
their faces on the ground and worship the
king when he appeared on the verandah of
the temple tower.

My readers will understand from what
has been said, how very important our Mission work must be in such great heathen
centres as Kandy. And the agency which is
likely to make the greatest impression on
the dense Buddhism of the Kandyan country
is, so I think, that which is carried on under
the auspices of the Ladies' Auxiliary Missionary Society, in our girls' schools, of
which we have now four; but we want ten
times as many.

All this by the way, however. You can imagine that our family party would be interested in the work of our Mission. It was not long before they were standing opposite the beautiful Methodist chapel in Brownrigg Street.

WESLEYAN CHAPEL.

And there for the first time in their lives they heard an organ. Gregoris was delighted, and when the organ blower laughingly gave him the bellows' handle to try it himself, he was amazed to find himself producing

such wonderful music.   For it seemed to him
at first that the organ blower was a much
more important man than the gentleman
who was there practising and sat leisurely
on a stool playing with the keys.   And when
it was explained to him, Gregoris thought he
would like to get a music box (for that was
what he called it) some day for their new
school chapel, and he would ask some English
lady to teach Punchi Nona to play it.

They were also very much interested, as
everybody is who sees it, in the ' traveller's
tree,' which spreads its great fan before the
chapel.   And Gregoris, who was getting to
regard himself as an educationist, paid a visit
to the school behind the chapel and picked
up information, which he intended should
be of some service to Nidigamma.

But the great event of their stay in
Kandy was, of course, the investment of the
*Muhandiram.*   It was the Queen's birthday
and a general holiday in Kandy.   Gregoris
had taken some hours to dress, or rather to
be dressed, that morning.   It was difficult
for him to get into his new semi-European
costume, and he did not feel at all at home
in his boots.   Poor Gregoris wished himself

in Nidigamma; it was easier going through the jungle than across the slippery floor of the Governor's reception room. In the midst of a very elaborate bow, which Gregoris had been practising for many days before, he would have fallen sprawling on the floor but

BUDDHIST PRIEST AND KANDYAN CHIEF.

for the timely help of an official who saw his difficulty.

Gregoris would have liked at that moment the privileged exemption from bowing permitted to the Buddhist priests who passed in before him with their shaven heads erect, who are supposed never to bow the head to any mortal. How the Kandyan chiefs managed it in all their finery and without losing their wonderful hats is a mystery.

The Governor, in conferring the honour, referred to what Gregoris had done for education in his village, and also said that there was nothing in the country that would be of such great and lasting benefit to it as a good system of female education in the villages. So you see that the little school which began with Punchi Nona for its first scholar was getting into notice in high quarters.

The *Muhandiram's* family and relatives treated the title for some time very much as boys will treat their first watch—they used it on all possible occasions. It was some weeks before our little party left Kandy for Nidigamma. But when they did go back they were received with such demonstrations of welcome as are rarely given even to the Government agent. Wonderful arches were erected. There was one at the school chapel which bore the inscription in letters of moss, placed there by Ratnaike—

WELCOME

TO THE NEW MUHANDIRAM.

And Gregoris felt a lump in his throat, and could only say, 'Very much obliged, my dears!' when the girls came out from the school-room and presented him with a beautifully bound copy of the Bible and Wesley's Hymns in Singhalese. Gregoris wore the costume which he had put on for the investment ceremony, including the belt and sword of office. He could scarcely manage to feel easy in all his pomp even yet; and as to the sword, he couldn't see the use of it to a quiet villager like himself. But Marihami liked it, and she had prevailed on Gregoris while in

Kandy, much against his will, to have his photograph taken,—in his uniform of course.

GREGORIS MUHANDIRAM.

In the evening of that day Gregoris gave a party: it was a party at which no intoxicating liquors were drunk. That was one of

the good things the school had been teaching
the people, that arrack and spirituous drinks
of any kind were injurious and did them
harm in every way ; so that as the school increased, the business at the village tavern
gradually decreased, until at last it was shut
up altogether.

You would have been amused if you could
have heard and understood Gregoris Muhandiram—we must not call him *Appu* now—
tell the story of his travels and adventures
that evening. To Nidigamma he was just
as much a hero as Stanley or any other distinguished African traveller is to us. He
told them of his investment. He described
the Governor and his surroundings. And
they looked with mingled feelings of awe
and reverence on the man who had got so
near the representative of Her Majesty the
Queen. But the description of the steam
engine on the railway, and the organ in the
chapel, brought their astonishment to its
height. They all agreed that it would be a
good thing to get a "music box" for their
school chapel. Ratnaike, who was present
at the entertainment, told Gregoris, after
the party broke up, that there was a good

L

girls' school in the town where he had been living, and he thought the lady in charge of it would not mind teaching Punchi Nona to play.

Punchi Nona's travels had taken a little conceit out of her and done her good. She was not *quite* perfect, you know, this young heroine of ours. And she had come back impressed with the fact that what she had acquired at Nidigamma looked very little after all when it was taken out into the big world for an airing.

# CHAPTER XII.

## NIDIGAMMA AWAKENED AND REFORMED.

WE have now come to the last chapter in this little story of female education and Singhalese village life; a story which is true of more places than Nidigamma, where the girls' schools are doing their blessed work. We skip over a great deal to get to this last chapter. A great deal might be said, for instance, of the big boarding-school in the town where Punchi Nona was trained as a teacher under the English lady sent out by the Ladies' Committee in London. But the two years spent there were full of incident, and a description of her experiences at the school would make a long story in itself.

There was one event, however, connected with that time which I must refer to. Punchi Nona always talks of it as the most important event in her life. She calls it her 'second birthday.' And I think you little boys and girls who have read the third chapter of St.

John's Gospel—and who has not?—will understand what she meant by it.

The English lady in charge of the big school thought it her duty to do something more than give the girls a good plain secular education. She knew that she was expected to lead the girls committed to her care to the Good Shepherd, and she aimed at doing that more than at securing a good grant by the Government examination; not simply because she was sent out for that purpose by the kind people of England, but because it was in her heart to do it. She talked frequently and lovingly with great earnestness to the girls about the change which our Saviour speaks of as the new birth. She told them that they could not see the kingdom of God unless they experienced this change of heart. They could not change themselves, as the Buddhists tried to do, by meditation and good works. God would change them in answer to prayer. He would give them the new heart which would love good things and love God.

She talked in this way frequently, and often prayed with the girls, because she knew that it was of the utmost importance that they should become true disciples of Jesus

Christ before they entered on the responsible
duties of teachers in the village schools.

It was a beautiful Sunday evening. The
boarders had just come back from the afternoon service in the adjoining chapel, where a
very zealous native Minister had been preaching. They gathered around the teacher in

the verandah of the boarding-house which
looked out over the calm, broad expanse of
the Indian Ocean. It was the sunset-time,
and a glorious sunset it was. The teacher
was looking at it in silence. She was probably thinking of the home she had left
beyond the golden rim of the sea. The girls

looked at it and thought of another home
—the heavenly home which the Minister had
been speaking about in the afternoon service.
They had been learning some of the English
hymns in the Sunday-school Hymn-book, and
Punchi Nona and one or two of the others
had actually learned to play a few simple tunes
on the harmonium, or the 'music box,' as
Gregoris Muhandiram called it.   And now as
they looked at all the glory of the sunset, one
of them recited the verse :—

> ' Jerusalem the golden,
>     When sunset's in the west,
>   It seems thy gate of glory,
>     Thou city of the blest ! '

'Yes,' said Punchi Nona, 'it is just
like it was when baby Gregoris went away.'
   ' Tell us about it,' said the teacher.   And
she told the story of her poor silly little brother
—the story which has already been given in
a previous chapter.
   Then they talked about the heavenly home
and the change of heart necessary before
entering that home.   And the teacher
said, 'Suppose we pray for the Lord Jesus to
come now and make us ready for His home.'

It was from that little prayer meeting on that Sabbath evening that Punchi Nona dated what she called her ' second birthday.'

One day, not long after, a messenger from Nidigamma arrived at the school with a message from the *Muhandiram* to say that Marihami was very ill, and Punchi Nona was wanted at home immediately. Poor Marihami was dying and she knew it. Her friends suggested a devil ceremony, but she said, ' No, I want to hear Punchi Nona pray ! '

· The old heathen leaven had gone, and the leaven of the village school, the leaven of the kingdom, which had been working for a long time in her dark mind, was manifesting blessed results. She told Sarnalis she knew she was leaving this life. ' The devil ceremony is sinful. It can do me no good, but I should like to hear Punchi Nona pray.'

It must be mentioned here that devil ceremonies had got by this time to be rather unusual things in Nidigamma, and I am sure Gregoris would not have allowed a dance in his house under any circumstances.

' Punchi Nona,' said Marihami very slowly, as she held her daughter's hand in the hot fever grasp of her own, ' tell me the story of the Beautiful Man, the Good Shepherd and the lost sheep, the story poor baby Gregoris liked so much.' Punchi Nona repeated the sweet story.

'Do you think He will come for me too, like He did for Gregoris?' she said.

Then the girl told her of the prayer meeting at the school and of the blessed change she had passed through. They prayed together, Punchi Nona kneeling by her mother's side, still grasping the hot hand. Gregoris sat near, looking at his daughter's kneeling form with as profound a reverence as ever priest was regarded with in the solemnity of the death-chamber. She, Marihami, passed away very quietly, saying she thought she had been too great a sinner for Jesus to take any notice, but the Good Shepherd was coming for her, just as He came for Gregoris. And the *Muhandiram* and his daughter were left in the room alone.

O my little English sisters, let me appeal to you on behalf of the thousands of the daughters of Ceylon who are dying without this hope, the perishing women whose lives are one dark night of ignorance and superstition, whose only light, in entering the darkness of the grave, is the torch of the devil priest.

Now we give another long skip, and we find the village of Nidigamma in a state of great excitement. The girls' school is again the centre of all the excitement. In the road leading up to the beautiful little school-chapel there are wonderful arches, with wonderful decorations, and on one of these arches you read in mossy letters, both English and Singhalese, ' *Welcome* to his Honour the Government Agent and Lady.' It is prize day again, and the Government Agent is expected to distribute the prizes. The chapel is crowded with children and grown-up people. On the platform, behind a table loaded with prizes, sit the Government Agent and his wife. Close to the platform in front of the audience sits an elderly-looking Singhalese gentleman in a long blue coat with very bright buttons, wearing the sash and sword of a *Muhandiram* of the Governor's Gate. It is our old friend Gregoris Appu. A handsome, intelligent young Singhalese Minister reads an address of welcome to the Agent in very good English, with just a few big words in it. The reader of the address is the Rev. Mr. Ratnaike,

M

who has just been received into the full
ministry of his Church and been appointed to
Nidigamma.    A bright-looking Singhalese
lady sits at a harmonium which leads the
singing part of the service.    You will say as
you look at her, 'Why it is Punchi Nona!'
No, it is not Punchi Nona.    This is Mrs.
Ratnaike, the mistress of the flourishing girls'
school of Nidigamma.    But she is the only
child of the old *Muhandiram*, and her name
*was* Punchi Nona.    She has become a *locu
nona* now, *i.e.*, a great lady, is the head of the
school, and plays the 'music box' in the
chapel.

The Agent made a speech in which he con-
trasted the Nidigamma of the old days with
the Nidigamma of to-day.    He spoke of the
change as a marvellous reform, and he
attributed it all to the working of the girls'
school; and he said that as long as he lived
he would encourage the establishment of
girls' schools in such places as Nidigamma.
Nidigamma had been thoroughly awakened
and deserved the name of 'sleep-village' no
longer.

When the Agent and his wife were leaving,
Mr. Ratnaike, with a bit of his old boyish

enthusiasm, shouted, 'Three cheers for the Government Agent.' Then after the cheering was over, the great man—the Agent—

MRS. RATNAIKE.

said, 'Now we'll have three cheers for the Nidigamma Girls' School and Mrs. Ratnaike, our old friend Punchi Nona, you know.' And didn't they cheer, that's all! The girls did it very solemnly, but the boys were uproarious. And Mrs. Ratnaike looked at the keys of the harmonium as if she had never counted the number of octaves before.

I think this will be an appropriate place to leave them. Facts and features which will be recognised in Ceylon have been woven into one continuous narrative in this simple story for the children of our Juvenile Associations and Busy Bees, to show them what a great work the Lord is doing by means of these girls' schools, which are so liberally supported by the members of such associations.

HAYMAN BROTHERS AND LILLY, HATTON HOUSE, 113, FARRINGDON ROAD, E.C.

# Standard & Popular Works

PUBLISHED BY

## T. WOOLMER, 2, CASTLE STREET, CITY ROAD, E.C.

## PRICE SIX SHILLINGS.

**The Light of the World: Lessons from the Life of Our Lord**
for Children. By the Rev. RICHARD NEWTON, DD., Author of *Rays from
the Sun of Righteousness*, etc., etc., etc. Fcap. 4to. Numerous Illusts.

'A most attractive and deeply interesting Sunday book for children.'

## PRICE FIVE SHILLINGS.

**Sermons by the Rev. W. MORLEY PUNSHON, LL.D.** With
a Preface by the Rev. W. ARTHUR, M.A. These Sermons contain the
latest Corrections of the Author. Two Volumes. Crown 8vo. 5/- each.

'Here we have found, in rare combination, pure and elevated diction,
conscience-searching appeal, withering exposure of sin, fearless advocacy of
duty, forceful putting of truth,' etc., etc.—*London Quarterly Review.*

**Lectures by the Rev. W. MORLEY PUNSHON, LL.D.**
Crown 8vo.

'One and all of the Lectures are couched in the powerful and popular style
which distinguished the great preacher, and they are worthy of a permanent
place in any library.'—*Daily Chronicle.*

**Toward the Sunrise: being Sketches of Travel in Europe**
and the East. To which is added a Memorial Sketch (with Portrait) of the
Rev. W. MORLEY PUNSHON, LL.D. By HUGH JOHNSTON, M.A., B.D.
Crown 8vo. Numerous Illustrations.

**Fiji and the Fijians; and Missionary Labours among the**
Cannibals. Sixth Thousand. Revised and Supplemented with Index. By
Rev. JAMES CALVERT; and a Preface by C. F. GORDON CUMMING, Author
of *At Home in Fiji*, etc. Crown 8vo, with Portrait of Thakombau, a Map,
and numerous Illustrations.

## PRICE FOUR SHILLINGS.

**Our Indian Empire: its Rise and Growth.** By the Rev.
J. SHAW BANKS. Imperial 16mo. Thirty-five Illustrations and Map.

'The imagination of the young will be fired by its stirring stories of English
victories, and it will do much to make history popular.'—*Daily Chronicle.*

'A well condensed and sensibly written popular narrative of Anglo-Indian
History.'—*Daily News.*

**Zoology of the Bible. By HARLAND COULTAS.** Preface
by the Rev. W. F. MOULTON, D.D. Imperial 16mo. 126 Illustrations.

'We have in a most convenient form all that is worth knowing of the
discoveries of modern science which have any reference to the animals
mentioned in Scripture.'—*Preacher's Budget.*

**Missionary Anecdotes, Sketches, Facts, and Incidents.**
By the Rev. WILLIAM MOISTER. Imperial 16mo. Eight Page Illustrations.

'The narratives are many of them very charming.'—*Sword and Trowel.*

12-84.

**Northern Lights; or, Pen and Pencil Sketches of Nineteen** Modern Scottish Worthies. By the Rev. J. MARRAT. Crown 8vo. Portraits and Illustrations.

'It is a charming book in every sense.'—*Irish Evangelist.*

**The Brotherhood of Men; or, Christian Sociology.** By Rev. W. UNSWORTH.

### PRICE THREE SHILLINGS AND SIXPENCE.

**Sabbath Chimes: A Meditation in Verse for the Sundays of a** Year. By Dr. PUNSHON. Crown 8vo, gilt edges.

**Uncle Jonathan's Walks in and Around London.** Foolscap 4to. Profusely Illustrated.

**Our Sea-Girt Isle: English Scenes and Scenery Delineated.** By the Rev. J. MARRAT. Imperial 16mo. Map and 153 Illustrations.

'An unusually readable and attractive book.'—*Christian World.*

**Rambles in Bible Lands.** By the Rev. RICHARD NEWTON, D.D. Imperial 16mo. Seventy Illustrations.

'From the juvenile stand-point, we can speak in hearty commendation of it.'—*Literary World.*

**'Land of the Mountain and the Flood':** Scottish Scenes and Scenery Delineated. By the Rev. JABEZ MARRAT. Imperial 16mo. Map and Seventy-six Illustrations.

'Described with taste, judgment, and accuracy of detail.'—*Scotsman.*

**Popery and Patronage.** Biographical Illustrations of Scotch Church History. By the Rev. J. MARRAT. Imperial 16mo. Ten Illustrations.

'Most instructive biographical narratives.'—*Derbyshire Courier.*

**Wycliffe to Wesley: Heroes and Martyrs of the Church in** Britain. Imperial 16mo. Twenty-four Portraits and Forty other Illustrations.

'We give a hearty welcome to this handsomely got up and interesting volume.'—*Literary World.*

**John Lyon; or, From the Depths.** By RUTH ELLIOTT. Crown 8vo. Five Full-page Illustrations.

'Earnest and eloquent, dramatic in treatment, and thoroughly healthy in spirit '—*Birmingham Daily Gazette.*

**The Thorough Business Man: Memoir of Walter Powell,** Merchant. By Rev. B. GREGORY. Seventh Edition. Crn. 8vo, with Portrait.

**The Life of Gideon Ouseley.** By the Rev. WILLIAM ARTHUR, M.A. Eighth Thousand. Crown 8vo, with Portrait.

**The Aggressive Character of Christianity.** By Rev. W. UNSWORTH.

**Garton Rowley; or, Leaves from the Log of a Master** Mariner. By J. JACKSON WRAY. Crown 8vo.

**Honest John Stallibrass.** By J. JACKSON WRAY. Crown 8vo.

**A Man Every Inch of Him.** By J. JACKSON WRAY. Cm. 8vo.

**Paul Meggitt's Delusion.** By J. JACKSON WRAY. Crown 8vo.

**Nestleton Magna.** A Story of Yorkshire Methodism. By J. JACKSON WRAY. Crown 8vo.

**Chronicles of Capstan Cabin; or, the Children's Hour.** By J. JACKSON WRAY. Imperial 16mo. Twenty-eight Illustrations.

**Missionary Stories, Narratives, Scenes, and Incidents.**
By the Rev. W. MOISTER. Crown 8vo. Eight Page Illustrations.
' Intensely interesting.'—*Methodist New Connexion Magazine.*

**Scenes and Adventures in Great Namaqualand.** By the
Rev. B. RIDSDALE. Crown 8vo, with Portrait.

**Melissa's Victory.** By ASHTON NEILL. Crown 8vo, gilt
edges. Illustrations by GUNSTON.

**Two Saxon Maidens.** By ELIZA KERR. Crown 8vo, gilt
edges. Illustrations by GUNSTON.

**Gems Reset ; or, the Wesleyan Catechisms Illustrated by**
Imagery and Narrative. Crown 8vo. By Rev. B. SMITH.

**Vice-Royalty ; or, a Royal Domain held for the King, and**
enriched by the King. Crown 8vo. Twelve page Illustns. By Rev. B. SMITH.

**Sunshine in the Kitchen ; or, Chapters for Maid Servants.**
Fourth Thousand. Crown 8vo. Numerous Illustrations. By Rev. B. SMITH.

**Way-Marks : Placed by Royal Authority on the King's**
Highway. Being One Hundred Scripture Proverbs, Enforced and Illustrated.
Crown 8vo. Eight Page Engravings. By Rev. B. SMITH.

**The Great Army of London Poor.** Sketches of Life and
Character in a Thames-side District By the River-side Visitor. Third
Edition. Crown 8vo. 540 pp. Eight Illustrations.
' Admirably told. The author has clearly lived and mingled with the
people he writes about.'—*Guardian.*

### PRICE TWO SHILLINGS AND SIXPENCE.

**Elias Power, of Ease-in-Zion.** By Rev. JOHN M. BAMFORD.
Fourth Thousand. Crown 8vo. Seventeen Illustrations. Gilt edges.

**Life of John Wicklif.** By Rev. W. L. WATKINSON. Portrait
and Eleven Illustrations. Crown 8vo.

**Good News for Children ; or, God's Love to the Little**
Ones. By JOHN COLWELL. Crown 8vo, gilt edges. Fourteen Illustrations.

**Pleasant Talks about Jesus.** By JOHN COLWELL. Crown 8vo.

**Little Abe ; or, the Bishop of Berry Brow.** Being the Life of
Abraham Lockwood, a quaint and popular Local Preacher. By F. JEWELL.
Crown 8vo, gilt edges. With Portrait.
' The racy, earnest, vernacular speech of *Little Abe*, and his quaint
illustrations and home-thrusts, are humorous indeed. . . . Cannot fail to be
a favourite.'—*Christian Age.*

**Cecily : a Tale of the English Reformation.** By EMMA LESLIE.
Crown 8vo. Five full-page Illustrations.
' This is an interesting and attractive little book. . . . It is lively and
healthy in tone.'—*Literary World.*

**Glimpses of India and Mission Life.** By Mrs. HUTCHEON.
Crown 8vo. Eight Page Illustrations.
' A well-written account of Indian life in its social aspects, by the wife of
an Indian missionary.'—*British Quarterly.*

**The Beloved Prince : a Memoir of His Royal Highness, the**
Prince Consort. By WILLIAM NICHOLS. Crown 8vo. With Portrait and
Nineteen Illustrations. Cloth, gilt edges.
' An admirable condensation of a noble life.'—*Derbyshire Courier.*

**Glenwood: a Story of School Life.** By JULIA K. BLOOM-FIELD. Crown 8vo. Seven Illustrations.

'A useful book for school-girls who think more of beauty and dress than of brains and grace.'—*Sword and Trowel.*

**Undeceived: Roman or Anglican?** A Story of English Ritualism. By RUTH ELLIOTT. Crown 8vo.

'In the creation and description of character the work belongs to the highest class of imaginative art.'—*Free Church of England Magazine.*

**Self-Culture and Self-Reliance, under God the Means of** Self-Elevation. By the Rev. W. UNSWORTH. Crown 8vo.

'An earnest, thoughtful, eloquent book on an important subject.'—*Folkestone News.*

**A Pledge that Redeemed Itself.** By SARSON, Author of 'Blind Olive,' etc. Crown 8vo. Numerous Illustrations. Gilt edges.

'We are informed in the preface that it is "an etching from life," and we can well believe it, for it bears all the marks of a genuine study of living men and women.'—*Literary World.*

**Old Daniel; or, Memoirs of a Converted Hindu.** By the Rev. T. HODSON. Crown 8vo, gilt edges. Coloured Illustrations.

**The Story of a Peninsular Veteran:** Sergeant in the 43rd Light Infantry during the Peninsular War. Crown 8vo. 13 Illustrations.

'Full of adventure, told in a religious spirit. We recommend this narrative to boys and young men.'—*Hastings and St. Leonard's News.*

**Rays from the Sun of Righteousness.** By the Rev. RICHARD NEWTON, D.D. Crown 8vo. Eleven Illustrations. Gilt edges.

**In the Tropics; or, Scenes and Incidents of West Indian Life.** By the Rev. JAMES MARRAT. Crown 8vo, gilt edges, Illustrations, etc.

'A vivid description of scenes and incidents, . . . with an interesting record of the progress of mission work.'—*Sheffield Post.*

**Climbing: a Manual for the Young who Desire to Rise in** Both Worlds. By the Rev. BENJAMIN SMITH. Crown 8vo. Sixth Edition.

**Our Visit to Rome, with Notes by the Way.** By the Rev. JOHN RHODES. Royal 16mo. Forty-five Illustrations.

**The Lancasters and their Friends.** A Tale of Methodist Life. By S. J. F. Crown 8vo.

**Those Boys.** By FAYE HUNTINGTON. Crown 8vo. Illustrated.

**Leaves from my Log of Twenty-five years' Christian** Work in the Port of London. Crown 8vo. Eight Illustrations.

**East End Pictures; or, More Leaves from My Log** of Twenty-five Years' Christian Work. By T. C. GARLAND. Crown 8vo. Portrait and Five Illustrations.

**The Willow Pattern: A Story Illustrative of Chinese Social** Life. By the Rev. HILDERIC FRIEND. Crown 8vo, gilt edges. Numerous Illustrations.

**Passages from the Diary of an Early Methodist.** By RICHARD ROWE.

**Orphans of the Forest; or, His Little Jonathan.** By A. E. COURTENAY. Foolscap 8vo. Four Illustrations.

## MARK GUY PEARSE'S WORKS.

*Nine Volumes, Crown 8vo, Cloth, Gilt Edges.    Price 2s. 6d. each.*

1.—Daniel Quorm, and his Religious Notions.    FIRST
SERIES. 70,000.

2.—Daniel Quorm, and his Religious Notions.    SECOND
SERIES. 22,000.

3.—Sermons for Children.    19,000.

4.—Mister Horn and his Friends; or, Givers and Giving.
21,000.

5.—Short Stories, and other Papers.    8000.

6.—'Good Will': a Collection of Christmas Stories.    9000.

7.—Simon Jasper.    11,000.

8.—Cornish Stories.    6000.

9.—Homely Talks.    11,000.

'Scarcely any living writer can construct a parable better, more quaintly,
simply, and congruously.  His stories are equally clever and telling. . . .
One secret of their spell is that they are brimful of heart. . . . His books
should be in every school library.'—*British Quarterly Review.*

Thoughts on Holiness.  By MARK GUY PEARSE.  Eleventh
Thousand.  Royal 16mo.  Cloth, red edges.

### PRICE TWO SHILLINGS.

Punchi Nona : A Story of Female Education and Village
Life in Ceylon.  By the Rev. SAMUEL LANGDON.  Crown 8vo.  Numerous
Illustrations.

Friends and Neighbours : A Story for Young Children.
Crown 8vo.  Illustrated.

The Oakhurst Chronicles : A Tale of the Times of Wesley.
By ANNIE E. KEELING.  Crown 8vo.  Four Illustrations.
'This beautiful story.'—*Sheffield Independent.*
'A fascinating story.'—*Christian Age.*

Poet Toilers in Many Fields.    By Mrs. R. A. WATSON.
Crown 8vo.  Thirteen Illustrations.

The 'Good Luck' of the Maitlands : a Family Chronicle.
By Mrs. R. A. WATSON.  Five Illustrations.  Crown 8vo.

Valeria, the Martyr of the Catacombs.  A Tale of Early
Christian Life in Rome.  By the Rev. W. H. WITHROW, D.D.  Crown 8vo.
Illustrations.

Tina and Beth; or, the Night Pilgrims.    By ANNIE
E. COURTENAY.  Crown 8vo.  Frontispiece.

Wilfred Hedley; or, How Teetotalism Came to Ellensmere.
By S. J. FITZGERALD.  Crown 8vo.  Frontispiece.

Equally Yoked: and other Stories.  By S. J. FITZGERALD.
Frontispiece.

Master and Man.  By S. J. FITZGERALD.  Frontispiece.

Coals and Colliers; or, How we Get the Fuel for our Fires.
By S. J. FITZGERALD.  Crown 8vo.  Illustrations.
'An interesting description of how we get the fuel for our fires, illustrated
by tales of miners' families.'—*Christian World.*

**James Daryll; or, From Honest Doubt to Christian Faith.**
By RUTH ELLIOTT. Crown 8vo.
'We have seldom read a more beautiful story than this.'—*The Echo.*

**The King's Messenger: a Story of Canadian Life. By the**
Rev. W. H. WITHROW, M.A. Crown 8vo.

**Illustrations of Fulfilled Prophecy. By the Rev. J. ROBINSON**
GREGORY. Crown 8vo. Numerous Illustrations.

**The Basket of Flowers. Illustrated. Crown 8vo, gilt edges.**

**The Great Apostle; or, Pictures from the Life of St. Paul.**
By the Rev. JABEZ MARRAT. Foolscap 8vo. 28 Illustrations and Map.
'A charming little book. . . . Written in a style that must commend itself
to young people.'—*Sunday-School Times.*

**Martin Luther, the Prophet of Germany. By the Rev. J.**
SHAW BANKS. Foolscap 8vo. 13 Illustrations.
'Mr. Banks has succeeded in packing a great deal of matter into a small
space, and yet has told his story in a very attractive style.'—*London
Quarterly Review.*

**Sir Walter Raleigh: Pioneer of Anglo-American Colonisation.**
By CHARLES K. TRUE, D.D. Foolscap 8vo. 16 Illustrations.
'We have here a book which we strongly recommend to our young readers.
It will do boys good to read it.'—*The Methodist.*

**Homes and Home Life in Bible Lands. By J. R. S.**
CLIFFORD. Foolscap 8vo. Eighty Illustrations.
'A useful little volume respecting the manners and customs of Eastern
nations. It brings together, in a small compass, much that will be of service
to the young student of the Bible.'—*Watchman.*

**Hid Treasures, and the Search for Them: Lectures to**
Bible Classes. By the Rev. J. HARTLEY. Foolscap 8vo. With Frontispiece.

**Youthful Obligations.** Illustrated by a large number of Appropriate Facts and Anecdotes. Foolscap 8vo. With Illustrations.

**Eminent Christian Philanthropists: Brief Biographical**
Sketches, designed especially as Studies for the Young. By the Rev.
GEORGE MAUNDER. Fcap. 8vo. Nine Illustrations.

**The Tower, the Temple, and the Minster: Historical and**
Biographical Associations of the Tower of London, St. Paul's Cathedral,
and Westminster Abbey. By the Rev. J. W. THOMAS. Second Edition.
Foolscap 8vo. 14 Illustrations.

**Peter Pengelly; or, 'True as the Clock.' By J. J. WRAY.**
Crown 8vo. Forty Illustrations.
'A famous book for boys.'—*The Christian.*

**The Stolen Children. By Rev. H. BLEBY. Foolscap 8vo.**
Six Illustrations.

**My Coloured Schoolmaster: and other Stories. By the Rev.**
H. BLEBY. Foolscap 8vo. Five Illustrations.
'The narratives are given in a lively, pleasant manner that is well suited to
gain and keep alive the attention of juvenile readers.'—*The Friend.*

**Female Heroism and Tales of the Western World. By**
the Rev. H. BLEBY. Foolscap 8vo. Four Illustrations.

**Capture of the Pirates: with other Stories of the Western Seas.**
By the Rev. HENRY BLEBY. Foolscap 8vo. Four Illustrations.
'The stories are graphically told, and will inform on some phases of
Western life.'—*Warrington Guardian.*

**The Prisoner's Friend:** The Life of Mr. JAMES BUNDY, of Bristol. By his Grandson, the Rev. W. R. WILLIAMS. Foolscap 8vo.

**Kilkee.** By ELIZA KERR, author of *Slieve Bloom.*

**Adelaide's Treasure, and How the Thief came Unawares.** By SARSON, Author of 'A Pledge that Redeemed Itself,' etc. Four Illustrations.
'This graphic story forms an episode in the history of Wesleyan Missions in Newfoundland.'—*Christian Age.*

**Two Snowy Christmas Eves.** By ELIZA KERR. Royal 16mo. Gilt edges. Six Illustrations.

PRICE EIGHTEENPENCE.

*'Little Ray' Series. Royal 16mo.*

**Little Ray and her Friends.** By RUTH ELLIOTT. Five Illustrations.

**The Breakfast Half-Hour:** Addresses on Religious and Moral Topics. By the Rev. H. R. BURTON. Twenty-five Illustrations.
'Practical, earnest, and forcible.'—*Literary World.*

**Gleanings in Natural History for Young People.** Profusely Illustrated.

**Broken Purposes; or, the Good Time Coming.** By LILLIE MONTFORT. Five Page Illustrations. Gilt edges.

**The History of the Tea-Cup:** with a Descriptive Account of the Potter's Art. By the Rev. G. R WEDGWOOD. Profusely Illustrated.

**The Cliftons and their Play-Hours.** By Mrs. COSSLETT. Seven Page Illustrations.

**The Lilyvale Club and its Doings.** By EDWIN A. JOHNSON, D.D. Seven Page Illustrations.
'The "doings" of the club decidedly deserve a careful perusal.'—*Literary World.*

**The Bears' Den.** By E. H. MILLER. Six Page Illustrations.
'A capital story for boys.'—*Christian Age.*

**Ned's Motto; or, Little by Little.** By the author of 'Faithful and True,' 'Tony Starr's Legacy.' Six Page Illustrations.
'The story of a boy's struggles to do right, and his influence over other boys. The book is well and forcibly written.'—*The Christian.*

**A Year at Riverside Farm.** By E. H. MILLER. Royal 16mo. Six Page Illustrations.
'A book of more than common interest and power.'—*Christian Age.*

**The Royal Road to Riches.** By E. H. MILLER. Fifteen Illustrations.

**Maude Linden; or, Working for Jesus.** By LILLIE MONTFORT. Four Illustrations.
'Intended to enforce the value of personal religion, especially in Christian work. . . . Brightly and thoughtfully written.'—*Liverpool Daily Post.*

**Oscar's Boyhood; or, the Sailor's Son.** By DANIEL WISE, D.D. Six Illustrations.
'A healthy story for boys, written in a fresh and vigorous style, and plainly teaching many important lessons.'—*Christian Miscellany.*

**Summer Days at Kirkwood.** By E. H. MILLER. Four Illustrations.

'Capital story; conveying lessons of the highest moral import.'—*Sheffield Post.*

**Slieve Bloom.** By ELIZA KERR, Author of *The Golden City*. Three Illustrations.

'The style of the book is graphic, and of considerable literary merit.'—*Literary World.*

'A real children's story, well told, with many beautiful touches of an artist's hand, and the evidences of a true woman's heart.'—*Christian Age.*

**Holy-days and Holidays;** or, Memories of the Calendar for Young People. By J. R. S. CLIFFORD. Numerous Illustrations.

'Instruction and amusement are blended in this little volume.—*The Christian.*

**Talks with the Bairns about Bairns.** By RUTH ELLIOTT. Illustrated.

'Pleasantly written, bright, and in all respects attractive.'—*Leeds Mercury.*

**My First Class:** and other Stories. By RUTH ELLIOTT. Illustrated.

'The stories are full of interest, well printed, nicely illustrated, and tastefully bound. It is a volume which will be a favourite in any family of children.'—*Derbyshire Courier.*

**Luther Miller's Ambition.** By LILLIE MONTFORT. Gilt edges. Illustrated by GUNSTON.

'*Wee Donald' Series.*' *Royal 16mo.*

**An Old Sailor's Yarn:** and other Sketches from Daily Life.

**The Stony Road:** a Tale of Humble Life.

**Stories for Willing Ears.** For Boys. By T. S. E.

**Stories for Willing Ears.** For Girls. By T. S. E.

**Thirty Thousand Pounds:** and other Sketches from Daily Life.

**'Wee Donald':** Sequel to 'Stony Road.'

PRICE EIGHTEENPENCE. *Foolscap 8vo Series.*

**Two Standard Bearers in the East:** Sketches of Dr. DUFF and Dr. Wilson. By Rev. J. MARRAT. Eight Illustrations.

**Three Indian Heroes:** the Missionary; the Soldier; the Statesman. By the Rev. J. SHAW BANKS. Numerous Illustrations.

**David Livingstone, Missionary and Discoverer.** By the Rev. J. MARRAT. Fifteen Page Illustrations.

'The story is told in a way which is likely to interest young people, and to quicken their sympathy with missionary work.'—*Literary World.*

**Columbus;** or, the Discovery of America. By GEORGE CUBITT. Seventeen Illustrations.

**Cortes;** or, the Discovery and Conquest of Mexico. By GEORGE CUBITT. Nine Illustrations.

**Pizarro;** or, the Discovery and Conquest of Peru. By GEORGE CUBITT. Nine Illustrations.

**Granada;** or, the Expulsion of the Moors from Spain. By GEORGE CUBITT. Seven Illustrations.

**James Montgomery, Christian Poet and Philanthropist.**
By the Rev. J. MARRAT. Eleven Illustrations.

'The book is a welcome and tasteful addition to our biographical knowledge.'—*Warrington Guardian.*

**The Father of Methodism: the Life and Labours of the Rev.**
John Wesley, A.M. By Mrs. COSSLETT. Forty-five Illustrations.

'Presents a clear outline of the life of the founder of Methodism, and is calculated to create a desire for larger works upon the subject. The illustrations are numerous and effective,—quite a pictorial history in themselves.'

**Old Truths in New Lights: Illustrations of Scripture Truth**
for the Young. By W. H. S. Illustrated.

**Chequer Alley: a Story of Successful Christian Work.** By
the Rev. F. W. BRIGGS, M.A.

**The Englishman's Bible: How he Got it, and Why he Keeps**
it. By the Rev. JOHN BOVES, M.A. Thirteen Illustrations.

**Home: and the Way to Make Home Happy.** By the Rev.
DAVID HAY. With Frontispiece.

**Helen Leslie; or, Truth and Error.** By ADELINE. Frontispiece.

**Building her House.** By Mrs. R. A. WATSON. Five Illustns.

'A charmingly written tale, illustrative of the power of Christian meekness.'
—*Christian World.*

**Crabtree Fold: a Tale of the Lancashire Moors.** By Mrs. R.
A. WATSON. Five Illustrations.

**Davy's Friend: and other Stories.** By JENNIE PERRETT.

'Excellent, attractive, and instructive.'—*The Christian.*

**Arthur Hunter's First Shilling.** By Mrs. CROWE.

**Hill Side Farm.** By ANNA J. BUCKLAND.

**The Boy who Wondered; or, Jack and Minnchen.** By Mrs.
GEORGE GLADSTONE.

**Kitty; or, The Wonderful Love.** By A. E. COURTENAY.
Illustrated.

**The River Singers.** By W. ROBSON.

PRICE EIGHTEENPENCE. *Crown 8vo Series.*

**Patty Thorne's Adventures.** By Mrs. H. B. PAULL. Illustrated.

**Fighting to Victory.** By EZEKIEL ROGERS. Second Edition.

**The Dairyman's Daughter.** By the Rev. LEGH RICHMOND,
M.A. A New Edition, with Additions, giving an Authentic Account of her Conversion, and of her connection with the Wesleyan Methodists.

**Footsteps in the Snow.** By ANNIE E. COURTENAY, Author
of *Tina and Beth,* etc., etc. Illustrated.

'Every page is genial, warm, and bright.'—*Irish Christian Advocate.*

**The Beloved Prince: A Memoir of His Royal Highness**
the Prince Consort. By WILLIAM NICHOLS. Nineteen Illustrations.

**Drierstock: A Tale of Mission Work on the American Frontier.**
Three Illustrations.

**Go Work: A Book for Girls.** By ANNIE FRANCES PERRAM.

**Picture Truths.** Practical Lessons on the Formation of Character, from Bible Emblems and Proverbs. By JOHN TAYLOR. Thirty Illustrations.

**Those Watchful Eyes; or, Jemmy and his Friends.** By EMILIE SEARCHFIELD. Frontispiece.

**The Basket of Flowers.** Four Illustrations.

**Auriel, and other Stories.** By RUTH ELLIOTT. Frontispiece.

**A Voice from the Sea; or, The Wreck of the Eglantine.** By RUTH ELLIOTT.

**Rays from the Sun of Righteousness.** By the Rev. R. NEWTON. Eleven Illustrations.

**A Pledge that Redeemed Itself.** By SARSON.
    'A clever, sparkling, delightful story.'—*Sheffield Independent.*

**In the Tropics; or, Scenes and Incidents of West Indian Life.** By the Rev. J. MARRAT. Illustrations and Map.

**Old Daniel; or, Memoirs of a Converted Hindu.** By Rev. T. HODSON. Twelve Illustrations.

**Little Abe; or, The Bishop of Berry-Brow.** Being the Life of Abraham Lockwood.

### CHEAP EDITION OF MARK GUY PEARSE'S BOOKS.

*Foolscap 8vo.   Price Eighteenpence each.*

1. **Daniel Quorm, and his Religious Notions.** 1ST SERIES.
2. **Daniel Quorm, and his Religious Notions.** 2ND SERIES.
3. **Sermons for Children.**
4. **Mister Horn and his Friends; or, Givers and Giving.**
5. **Short Stories: and other Papers.**
6. **' Good Will': a Collection of Christmas Stories.**

### PRICE ONE SHILLING. *Imperial 32mo. Cloth, gilt lettered.*

**Abbott's Histories for the Young.**
    Vol. 1. Alexander the Great. Vol. 2. Alfred the Great. Vol. 3. Julius Cæsar.

### PRICE ONE SHILLING. *Royal 16mo. Cloth, gilt lettered.*

**Ancient Egypt: Its Monuments, Worship, and People.** By the Rev. EDWARD LIGHTWOOD. Twenty-six Illustrations.

**Vignettes from English History.** From the Norman Conqueror to Henry IV. Twenty-three Illustrations.

**Margery's Christmas Box.** By RUTH ELLIOTT. Seven Illusts.

**No Gains without Pains: a True Life for the Boys.** By H. C. KNIGHT. Six Illustrations.

**Peeps into the Far North: Chapters on Iceland, Lapland, and Greenland.** By S. E. SCHOLES. Twenty-four Illustrations.

**Lessons from Noble Lives, and other Stories.** 31 Illustrations.

Stories of Love and Duty. For Boys and Girls. 31 Illusts.

The Railway Pioneers; or, the Story of the Stephensons, Father and Son. By H.C. KNIGHT. Fifteen Illustrations.

The Royal Disciple: Louisa, Queen of Prussia. By C.R. HURST. Six Illustrations.

Tiny Tim: a Story of London Life. Founded on Fact. By F. HORNER. Twenty-two Illustrations.

John Tregenoweth. His Mark. By MARK GUY PEARSE. Twenty-five Illustrations.

'I'll Try'; or, How the Farmer's Son became a Captain. Ten Illustrations.

The Giants, and How to Fight Them. By Dr. RICHARD NEWTON. Fifteen Illustrations.

The Meadow Daisy. By LILLIE MONTFORT. Numerous Illustrations.

Robert Dawson; or, the Brave Spirit. Four Page Illustrations.

The Tarnside Evangel. By M. A. H. Eight Illustrations.

Rob Rat: a Story of Barge Life. By MARK GUY PEARSE. Numerous Illustrations.

The Unwelcome Baby, with other Stories of Noble Lives early Consecrated. By S. ELLEN GREGORY. Nine Illustrations.

Jane Hudson, the American Girl. Four Page Illustrations.

The Babes in the Basket; or, Daph and her Charge. Four Page Illustrations.

Insect Lights and Sounds. By J. R. S. CLIFFORD. Illustrns.
'A valuable little book for children, pleasantly illustrated.'—*The Friend.*

The Jew and his Tenants. By A. D. WALKER. Illustrated.
'A pleasant little story of the results of genuine Christian influence.'—*Christian Age.*

The History of Joseph: for the Young. By the Rev. T. CHAMPNESS. Twelve Illustrations.
'Good, interesting, and profitable.'—*Wesleyan Methodist Magazine.*

The Old Miller and his Mill. By MARK GUY PEARSE. Twelve Illustrations.

The First Year of my Life: a True Story for Young People. By ROSE CATHAY FRIEND.
'It is a most fascinating story.'—*Sunday School Times.*

Fiji and the Friendly Isles: Sketches of their Scenery and People. By S. E. SCHOLES. Fifteen Illustrations.
'We warmly recommend this little volume to readers of every sort.'—*Hastings and St. Leonard's News.*

The Story of a Pillow. Told for Children. Four Illustrations.
'Simply and gracefully told.'—*Bradford Observer.*
'Little folks are sure to be interested in this wonderful pillow.'—*Literary World.*

## UNCLE DICK'S LIBRARY OF SHILLING BOOKS.

*Foolscap 8vo. 128 pp. Cloth.*

**Uncle Dick's Legacy.** By E. H. MILLER, Author of 'Royal Road to Riches,' etc., etc. Illustrated.
'A first-rate story . . . full of fun and adventure, but thoroughly good and healthy.'—*Christian Miscellany.*

**Beatrice and Brian.** By HELEN BRISTON. Three Illustrns.
'A very prettily told story about a wayward little lady and a large mastiff dog, specially adapted for girls.'—*Derbyshire Advertiser.*

**Becky and Reubie; or, the Little Street Singers.** By MINA E. GOULDING. Three Illustrations.
'A clever, pleasing, well-written story.'—*Leeds Mercury.*

**Gilbert Guestling; or, the Story of a Hymn Book.** Illustrated.
'It is a charmingly told story.'—*Nottingham Daily Express.*

**Guy Sylvester's Golden Year.** Three Illustrations.
'A very pleasantly written story.'—*Derbyshire Courier.*

**Left to Take Care of Themselves.** By A. RYLANDS. Three Illustrations.

**Tom Fletcher's Fortunes.** By Mrs. H. B. PAULL. Three Illustrations.
'A capital book for boys.'—*Sheffield and Rotherham Independent.*

**The Young Bankrupt, and other Stories.** By Rev. JOHN COLWELL. Three Illustrations.

**The Basket of Flowers.** Four Illustrations.

**Mattie and Bessie; or, Climbing the Hill.** By A. E. COURTENAY.

**Tom: A Woman's Work for Christ.** By Rev. J. W. KEYWORTH. Six Illustrations.

**The Little Disciple: The Story of his Life Told for Young Children.** Six Illustrations.

**Afterwards.** By EMILIE SEARCHFIELD. Three Page Illustns.

---

**Mischievous Foxes; or, the Little Sins that mar the Christian Character.** By JOHN COLWELL. Price 1s.
'An amazing amount of sensible talk and sound advice.'—*The Christian.*

**Joel Bulu: The Autobiography of a Native Minister in the South Seas.** New Edition, with an account of his Last Days. Edited by the Rev. G. S. ROWE. Foolscap 8vo, cloth. Price 1s.

**Robert Moffat, the African Missionary.** By Rev. J. MARRAT. Foolscap 8vo, Illustrated. Price 1s.

**The Dairyman's Daughter.** By the Rev. LEGH RICHMOND, M.A. A New Edition, with Additions, giving an Authentic Account of her Conversion, and of her connection with the Wesleyan Methodists.

**Polished Stones from a Rough Quarry.** By Mrs. HUTCHEON. Price 1s.
'A Scotch story of touching and pathetic interest. It illustrates the power of Christian sympathy.'—*Irish Evangelist.*

**Recollections of Methodist Worthies.** Fcap 8vo. Price 1s.
'Deserves to be perused by members of all Christian communities.'—*Sword and Trowel.*

**PRICE NINEPENCE.** *Imperial 32mo. Cloth, Illuminated.*

1. The Wonderful Lamp : and other Stories.   By RUTH ELLIOTT.  Five Illustrations.
2. Dick's Troubles : and How He Met Them.   By RUTH ELLIOTT.  Six Illustrations.
3. The Chat in the Meadow : and other Stories.  By LILLIE MONTFORT.  Six Illustrations.
4. John's Teachers : and other Stories.  By LILLIE MONT-FORT.  Six Illustrations.
5. Nora Grayson's Dream : and other Stories.  By LILLIE MONTFORT.  Seven Illustrations.
6. Rosa's Christmas Invitations : and other Stories.  By LILLIE MONTFORT.  Six Illustrations.
7. Ragged Jim's Last Song : and other Ballads.  By EDWARD BAILEY.  Eight Illustrations.
8. Pictures from Memory. By ADELINE.  Nine Illustrations.
9. The Story of the Wreck of the 'Maria' Mail Boat : with a Memoir of Mrs. Hincksman, the only Survivor.  Illustrated.
10. Passages from the Life of Heinrich Stilling.  Five Page Illustrations.
11. Little and Wise : The Ants, The Conies, The Locusts, and the Spiders.  Twelve Illustrations.
12. Spoiling the Vines, and Fortune Telling.  Eight Illusts.
13. The Kingly Breaker, Concerning Play, and Sowing the Seed.
14. The Fatherly Guide, Rhoda, and Fire in the Soul.
15. Short Sermons for Little People.   By the Rev. T. CHAMPNESS.
16. Sketches from my Schoolroom.  Four Illustrations.
17. Mary Ashton : A True Story of Eighty Years Ago.  4 Illusts.
18. The Little Prisoner : or, the Story of the Dauphin of France.  Five Illustrations.
19. The Story of an Apprenticeship.  By the Rev. A. LANGLEY.  Frontispiece.
20. Mona Bell : or, Faithful in Little Things.  By EDITH M. EDWARDS.  Four Illustrations.
21. Minnie Neilson's Summer Holidays, and What Came of Them.  By M. CAMBWELL.  Four Illustrations.
22. After Many Days ; or, The Turning Point in James Power's Life.  Three Illustrations.
23. Alfred May.  By R. RYLANDS.  Two coloured Illustrations.
24. Dots and Gwinnie : a Story of Two Friendships.  By R. RYLANDS.  Three Illustrations.
25. Little Sally.  By MINA E. GOULDING.  Six Illustrations.
26. Joe Webster's Mistake.   By EMILIE SEARCHFIELD.  Three Illustrations.
27. Muriel ; or, The Sister Mother.
28. Nature's Whispers.
29. Johnny's Work and How he did it.  Five Illustrations.
30. Pages from a Little Girl's Life.  By A. F. PERRAM.  Five Illustrations.
31. The Wrens' Nest at Wrenthorpe. By A. E. KEELING.  Five Illustrations.

**PRICE EIGHTPENCE.** *Imperial 32mo. Cloth, gilt edges.*

The whole of the Ninepenny Series are also sold in Limp Cloth at Eightpence.

Ancasa, the Slave Preacher. By the Rev. HENRY BUNTING.

Bernard Palissy, the Huguenot Potter. By A. E. KEELING.

Brief Description of the Principal Places mentioned in Holy Scripture.

Bulmer's History of Joseph.

Bulmer's History of Moses.

Christianity Compared with Popery : A Lecture.

Death of the Eldest Son (The). By CÆSAR MALAN.

Emily's Lessons ; Chapters in the Life of a Young Christian.

Fragments for Young People.

Freddie Cleminson.

Janie : A Flower from South Africa.

Jesus (History of). For Children. By W. MASON.

Little Nan's Victory. By A. E. COURTENAY.

Martin Luther (The Story of).

Precious Seed, and Little Sowers.

Recollections of Methodist Worthies. Foolscap 8vo, limp cloth.

Sailor's (A) Struggles for Eternal Life.

Saville (Jonathan), Memoirs of. By the Rev. F. A. WEST.

Soon and Safe : A Short Life well Spent.

Sunday Scholar's Guide (The). By the Rev J. T. BARR.

The Wreck, Rescue, and Massacre : an Account of the Loss of the *Thomas King*.

Will Brown ; or, Saved at the Eleventh Hour. By the Rev. H. BUNTING.

Youthful Sufferer Glorified : A Memorial of Sarah Sands Hay.

Youthful Victor Crowned : A Sketch of Mr. C. JONES.

**THE CROWN SERIES.** *16mo. Cloth, gilt lettered. Coloured Frontispiece.* **PRICE SIXPENCE.**

1. A Kiss for a Blow : true Stories about Peace and War for Children.
2. Louis Henrie ; or, The Sister's Promise.
3. The Giants, and How to Fight Them.
4. Robert Dawson ; or, the Brave Spirit.
5. Jane Hudson, the American Girl.
6. The Jewish Twins. By Aunt FRIENDLY.
7. The Book of Beasts. 35 Illust.
8. The Book of Birds. 40 Illust.
9. Proud in Spirit.
10. Althea Norton.
11. Gertrude's Bible Lesson.
12. The Rose in the Desert.
13. The Little Black Hen.
14. Martha's Hymn.
15. Nettie Mathieson.
16. The Prince in Disguise.
17. The Children on the Plains.
18. The Babes in the Basket.
19. Richard Harvey ; or, Taking a Stand.
20. Kitty King : Lessons for Little Girls.
21. Nettie's Mission.
22. Little Margery.
23. Margery's City Home.
24. The Crossing Sweeper.
25. Rosy Conroy's Lessons.
26. Ned Dolan's Garret.
27. Little Henry and his Bearer.
28. The Little Woodman and his Dog.
29. Johnny : Lessons for Little Boys.
30. Pictures and Stories for the Little Ones.
31. A Story of the Sea : and other Incidents.
32. Aunt Lizzie's Talks about Remarkable Fishes. 40 Illusts.
33. Three Little Folks who Mind their own Business ; or, The Bee, the Ant, and the Spider. 25 Illustrations.

The whole of the above thirty-three Sixpenny books are also sold at Fourpence, in Enamelled Covers.

## PRICE SIXPENCE. 18mo. *Cloth, gilt lettered.*

African Girls; or, Leaves from the Journal of a Missionary's Widow.
Bunyan (John). The Story of his Life and Work told to Children. By E. M. C.
Celestine; or, the Blind Woman of the Pastures.
Christ in Passion Week; or, Our Lord's last Public Visit to Jerusslem.
Crown with Gems (The). A Call to Christian Usefulness.
Fifth of November; Romish Plotting for Popish Ascendency.
Flower from Feejee. A Memoir of Mary Calvert.
Good Sea Captain (The). Life of Captain Robert Steward.
Grace the Preparation for Glory: Memoir of A. Hill. By Rev. J. RATTENBURY.
Joseph Peters, the Negro Slave.

Hattie and Nancy; or, the Everlasting Love. A Book for Girls.
Held Down; or, Why James did Not Prosper.
Matt Stubbs' Dream: A Christmas Story. By M. G. PEARSE.
Michael Faraday. A Book for Boys.
Our Lord's Public Ministry.
Risen Saviour (The).
St. Paul (Life of).
Seed for Waste Corners. By Rev. B. SMITH.
Sorrow on the Sea; or, the Loss of the *Amazon*.
Street (A) I've Lived in. A Sabbath Morning Scene.
Three Naturalists: Stories of Linnæus, Cuvier, and Buffon.
Young Maid-Servants (A Book for). Gilt Edges.

## PRICE FOURPENCE. *Enamelled Covers.*

Precious Seed, and Little Sowers.
Spoiling the Vines.
Rhoda, and Fire in the Soul.
The Fatherly Guide, and Fortune Telling.
Will Brown; or, Saved at the Eleventh Hour.

Ancass, the Slave Preacher. By the Rev. H. BUNTING.
Bernard Palissy, the Huguenot Potter.
The Story of Martin Luther. By Rev. J. B. NORTON.
Little Nan's Victory.

The whole of the thirty-three books in the Crown Series at Sixpence are sold in Enamelled Covers at FOURPENCE each.

## PRICE THREEPENCE. *Enamelled Covers.*

'The Ants' and 'The Conies.'
Concerning Play.
'The Kingly Breaker' and 'Sowing the Seed.'
'The Locusts' and 'The Spiders.'
Hattie and Nancy.
Michael Faraday.
John Bunyan. By E. M. C.

Three Naturalists: Stories of Linnæus, Cuvier, and Buffon.
Celestine; or, the Blind Woman of the Pastures.
Held Down; or, Why James didn't Prosper. By Rev. B. SMITH.
The Good Sea Captain. Life of Captain Robert Steward.

## PRICE TWOPENCE. *Enamelled Covers.*

1. The Sun of Righteousness.
2. The Light of the World.
3. The Bright and Morning Star.
4. Jesus the Saviour.
5. Jesus the Way.
6. Jesus the Truth.
7. Jesus the Life.
8. Jesus the Vine.
9. The Plant of Renown.

10. Jesus the Shield.
11. Being and Doing Good. By the Rev. J COLWELL.
12. Jessie Allen's Question.
13. Uncle John's Christmas Story.
14. The Pastor and the Schoolmaster.
15. Laura Gaywood.

*The above Twopenny Books are also sold in Packets.*
Packet No. 1, containing Nos. 1 to 6, Price 1/-
Packet No. 2, containing Nos. 7 to 12, Price 1/-

PRICE ONE PENNY. *New Series. Royal 32mo. With Illustrations.*

1. The Woodman's Daughter. By LILLIE M.
2. The Young Pilgrim : the Story of Louis Jaulmea.
3. Isaac Watkin Lewis : a Life for the Little Ones. By MARK GUY PEARSE.
4. The History of a Green Silk Dress.
5. The Dutch Orphan : Story of John Harmsen.
6. Children Coming to Jesus. By Dr. CROOK.
7. Jesus Blessing the Children. By Dr. CROOK.
8. 'Under Her Wings.' By the Rev. T. CHAMPNESS.
9. 'The Scattered and Peeled Nation': a Word to the Young about the Jews.
10. Jessie Morecambe and Her Playmates.
11. The City of Beautiful People.
12. Ethel and Lily's School Treat. By R. R.

The above twelve books are also sold in a Packet, price 1/-

## NEW SERIES OF HALFPENNY BOOKS.

By MARK GUY PEARSE, LILLIE MONTFORT, RUTH ELLIOTT, and others. *Imperial 32mo. 16 pages. With Frontispiece.*

1. The New Scholar.
2. Is it beneath You?
3. James Elliott; or, the Father's House.
4. Rosa's Christmas Invitations.
5. A Woman's Ornaments.
6. 'Things Seen and Things not Seen.'
7. Will you be the Last?
8. 'After That !'
9. Christmas; or, the Birthday of Jesus.
10. The School Festival.
11. John's Teachers.
12. Whose Yoke do You Wear?
13. The Sweet Name of Jesus.
14. My Name; or, How shall I Know?
15. Annie's Conversion.
16. The Covenant Service.
17. The Chat in the Meadow.
18. The Wedding Garment.
19. 'Love Covereth all Sins.'
20. Is Lucy V——— Sincere?
21. He Saves the Lost.
22. The One Way.
23. Nora Grayson's Dream.
24. The Scripture Tickets.
25. 'Almost a Christian.'
26. 'Taken to Jesus.'
27. The New Year; or, Where shall I Begin?
28. The Book of Remembrance.
29. 'Shall we Meet Beyond the River?'
30. Found after Many Days.
31. Hugh Coventry's Thanksgiving.
32. Our Easter Hymn.
33. 'Eva's New Year's Gift.'
34. Noble Impulses.
35. Old Rosie. By MARK GUY PEARSE.
36. Nellie's Text Book.
37. How Dick Fell out of the Nest.
38. Dick's Kitten.
39. Why Dick Fell into the River.
40. What Dick Did with his Cake.
41. Dick's First Theft.
42. Dick's Revenge.
43. Alone on the Sea.
44. The Wonderful Lamp.
45. Not too Young to Understand.
46. Being a Missionary.
47. Willie Rowland's Decision.
48. 'Can it Mean Me?'
49. A Little Cake.
50. A Little Coat.
51. A Little Cloud.
52. The Two Brothers : Story of a Lie. By MARK GUY PEARSE.

*The above Series are also sold in Packets.*

Packet No. 1 contains Nos. 1 to 24.   Price 1/-
Packet No. 2 contains Nos. 25 to 48.   Price 1/-

LONDON:
T. WOOLMER, 2, CASTLE STREET, CITY ROAD, E.C.

CPSIA information can be obtained
at www.ICGtesting.com
Printed in the USA
BVOW07s2328310716
457487BV00003B/12/P